What People are Saying

Rev. Arthur Ellison, Founder & President, 2nd Question
"Maria's daily readings are as fresh, real, convicting and comforting as you will find anywhere. They are like small pieces of amazing chocolate that you want to savor and enjoy for as long as you can. I often found myself looking ahead to the next day's reading because today's was so unbelievably delicious."

Mrs. Letty K. Peterson,
Owner of Heavenly Housekeeping & Photography
"I love Maria's daily devotionals because they are true to life. I'm able to relate to them and be encouraged by them in the morning with my cup of coffee before heading out into my day. They have helped me through one of the hardest times in my life. I have difficulty sharing, but because of Maria's example, I've stepped out of my comfort zone and have begun sharing my story with others. I love Maria's heart and I am grateful that God has placed her in my life."

Rev. Glen Schreiber, Southeast District Superintendent,
The Evangelical Free Church of America
"Life is a journey, so walk it with someone you like. I like Maria. You will, too. Enjoy your time with her (and her God!) each day. You'll look forward to tomorrow. Sometimes I peek!"

Mrs. Jennifer Lee, Founder & CEO of Cornerstone Strategic Group
"Maria Belyea has an amazing gift for sharing the message of Jesus through life lessons and everyday stories to which we can all relate. Missing one of her inspirational stories is like missing a visit from a dear friend, it leaves me disappointed for the day, but anxiously anticipating tomorrow's encouragement."

Dr. Dave White, International Success Life Coach, NCAA Men's Basketball Lead Referee, & Senior Pastor at The Bridge Church
"Ever need a brief word of encouragement, a quick pick-me-up, a "you-got-this" affirmation to get your heart and head straight for the duties of the day? *Little Seeds of Hope* is a perfect punch of

positivity and practicality. Women will find it conversational and uplifting. Men will find it practical and relatable. I know you'll enjoy the much-needed hope Maria extends to us all."

Mrs. Heather Woolf, RN,
Regional Administrator for Activa Home Health
"In a world where at every turn women are told they are not enough, Maria's tales of encouragement bring hope and healing. She shares the raw and real moments of life, and turns each into delicious morsels of inspiration and hope. Expect tears, laughter, and a connection to every woman's life story."

Rev. Mike Chong Perkins, Lead Pastor at Crossroads Christian Fellowship, Big Fork, MT & Lead Developer at The Praxis Center for Church Development
"What a delightful book Maria has written! Refreshingly honest, bold with conviction about the God who heals and gives hope and wonderfully practical for daily living. In our day and age where knowledge is easy accessable via the internet, it is wonderful to feel the cool breeze of refreshing wisdom that flows from Maria's life. Her transparency brings hope and helps the reader understand how little seeds of hope can grow into mighty oaks of righteousness."

Rev. Fritz Dale, National Director of Leadership Development & Prayer Mobilization for The Evangelical Free Church of America
"Maria Belyea speaks and writes as one who has journeyed with the Lord down many adventure filled trails. Her insightful and encouraging daily devotions capture the heart of God and motivate one to follow after Him. This is a powerful resource for people of all ages and stages of life, men and women, those who follow Jesus and those who are looking for him."

Dr. John Kimball, Lead Pastor of Palmwood Church, Oviedo, Florida, & Director of Church Development for the Conservative Congregational Christian Conference

"Everyone needs encouragement. My friend Maria Belyea takes everyday scenarios from her personal walk with Jesus and applies the Word of God to provide a daily nugget of encouraging application for each of us. It's a great way to start off your busy day, to get a quick moment with God at lunch, or to settle in before bed. It'll be a blessing to you!"

Rev. Alan Kraft, Lead Pastor of Christ Community Church, Greely, CO. Author of *More: When A Little Bit of the Spirit is Not Enough*, and *Good News for Those Trying Harder*

"Stories are the access point to the heart, which is why this book is such a wonderful resource. In *Little Seeds of Hope*, Maria beautifully reminds us how God meets us in the day to day experiences of life. Read this book and your soul will be encouraged!"

Dr. Casey Cleveland,
Lead Pastor of The Avenue Church, Delray Beach, FL.

"*Little Seeds of Hope* is an encouraging recipe of gospel truth, practical example, and inviting narrative. Not only will this journey point you to Jesus, but expect your heart to smile along the way. May the God of grace visit you in a special way throughout these one hundred days!"

Dr. Kevin Kompelien, President,
The Evangelical Free Church of America

"The everyday things of life are often what trip us up as we seek to live for Jesus. Discouragement, doubt and distractions rob us of the joy the Lord intended for our lives. In *Little Seeds of Hope* Maria Belyea gives us glimpses into the everyday issues she and her family face. With a genuine trust in Jesus, based on the timeless truth of the Scriptures, these real-life stories bring hope for the challenging things we face, deepening our faith and strengthening our commitment to live for Jesus."

Mrs. Heather Diebler, PA-C and Wellness Provider
"A day with Maria Belyea's *Little Seeds of Hope* is a better day. Living in South Korea during a challenging season, I have eagerly looked forward to reading Maria's posts every evening. A masterful story-teller, Maria has a way of piercing into the depths of my heart with her devotions and encouraging me to grow. Her transparency reminds me that we all have common struggles and Jesus is the Hope that allows us to transform from a planted seed into a flourishing, strong, lovely tree."

Dr. Tom Johnston, Lead Pastor of Trinity Life Community Church, Bedford, NH, Co-founder & Executive Director of The Praxis Center for Church Development
"The Apostle Paul said that he "press(ed) on toward the goal for the prize of the upward call of God in Christ Jesus." (Philippians 3:14 ESV) Such "pressing on" can only occur through daily engagement with the Lord. Our devotional life and the practice of spiritual disciplines are essential elements in our engagement with Him, providing opportunity for the Holy Spirit to reveal His will for us and to guide us in His way. Devotionals are key tools for our daily pursuit of Christ and His Kingdom purposes for us. They provide comfort, insight, encouragement, and at times, much needed exhortation to get up and get moving - and keep moving - with Jesus. To that end, Maria Belyea has succeeded brilliantly with this devotional, giving the body of Christ a practical and accessible tool for pursuing Jesus, one which I can highly recommend to any who seek to press on into His Kingdom way of life."

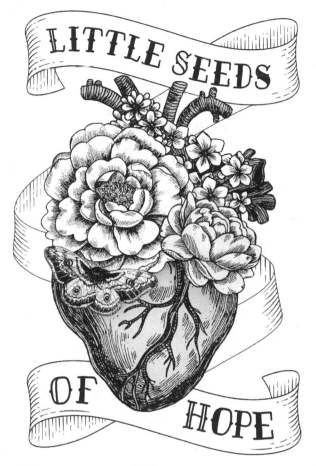

LITTLE SEEDS OF HOPE

100 Days of Encouragement

MARIA BELYEA

LITTLE SEEDS OF HOPE

© Copyright 2018 by Maria Belyea

ISBN: 978-0-911802-10-8

All Scripture quotations unless marked are taken from the Holy Bible, New International Version®, NIV®. Copyright © 1973, 1978, 1984, 2011 by Biblica, Inc.™ Used by permission of Zondervan. All rights reserved worldwide. www.zondervan.com The "NIV" and "New International Version" are trademarks registered in the United States Patent and Trademark Office by Biblica, Inc.™

Published in the United States of America by:

Next Step Resources
7890 12th Ave South, Bloomington, MN 55425

www.nsresources.com

1 (800) 444-2665

Book layout, design and format by Kim Gardell, Gardell Design

ACKNOWLEDGEMENTS

Thank you Foye Belyea for agreeing to have coffee with me
25 years ago, making the bed every morning,
letting me have small, annoying little dogs,
praying for me every day and keeping me supplied with chocolate.
You are my favorite.

Cover Design: Julie Fries and Jennifer Mateo

Editing: Deneen Parker

Hair and Makeup: Courtesy of Bethany Bartlett Tomko (owner and
stylist) and Liz Hunter (stylist),
Purstrands Salon, Boca Raton, Florida

Photography credit: Nicolette Sowers

INTRODUCTION

I was living the life of a hypocrite. I was leading worship at church on Sundays and talking about how awesome God is, but not living it out the rest of the week. Overwhelmed and constantly stressed, my prayers were all about giving God the laundry list of things He needed to fix and then begging Him to fix them, immediately. My life was low on joy and full of anxiety.

The truth is that just because I'm married to a pastor, it doesn't mean I wake up like Snow White with little birds chirping over my head as I stretch, yawn, and sing in an angelic voice, "Good Morning God! I'm going to read the Bible now!" Yeah, not so much. I hate getting up in the morning. My husband Foye, would often make coffee to try and lure me out of bed. I'd much rather stay up late, get things done while the house is quiet and then sleep in. Along with being a pastor's wife, I'm a mom and a full time Registered Nurse. I barely have time to shower and brush my teeth, let alone read the Bible.

Then, about a year and a half ago we moved to Florida and I stumbled upon a church that was started for addicts, although you don't have to be an addict to go there. It's the coolest, most real church I've ever been in and I've been in a lot of churches. It was planted to bring hope to all the people that come to South Florida for treatment and a new life, a fresh start. Our pastor looks like a skateboarder, as if he'd be more comfortable dropping in the half-pipe at the X games than preaching behind a pulpit. The first day something clicked. These are my people! I've never done drugs. I've never even smoked a cigarette, at least not a whole one (I took a puff once and it burned my throat, and that was the end of that). I am a food addict. I used to weigh close to 270 pounds. I know what it is like to be completely in the grip of addiction and hate yourself and feel like nothing is EVER going to change.

In January 2018, our pastor started a sermon series on what it means to be "ALL IN." I had just finished leading worship and was sitting in the back of the church, when I heard him say that part of being ALL IN this year meant giving the first three minutes of your day to God. My first thoughts were – YES! I can do this. I need to do this. I don't want to be a hypocrite. I'm up there leading worship every week and I need to be on board one hundred percent with our church's mission. Then he suggested downloading a Bible app to send you a verse of the day. He wanted us to read that verse, pray and then send it out to three other people to encourage them.

I decided to set my alarm five minutes earlier than normal and read my verse before I even got out of bed. I said a little prayer and texted it to three other people. Then I began to think, I have a lot of Facebook friends, what if I posted my verse to Facebook? Maybe I could encourage twenty people! I started exploring the Bible app I had downloaded and realized it was pretty cool! They have these themed daily readings on all kinds of topics and you get to check off little boxes when you're done. I LOVE checking off little boxes! Before I knew it, I was setting my alarm twenty minutes early because I didn't want to ruin my streak.

I confess, I'm not one of those people who can eat one little square of a candy bar and put the rest in my pocket for later. I LOVE chocolate and that candy bar would burn a hole in my pocket. It would become all I could think about until I inhaled the rest. That's how three minutes with God felt to me, like a tiny taste of chocolate that left me wanting more. I used to think I didn't have time for God. Now, I can't imagine starting my day any other way.

By the time February came I was on a roll checking off my little boxes when I had what I thought was a brilliant idea! I turned to my husband and said, "Foye, YOU should write a daily devotional for Lent (for non churchy people - that's the forty days before Easter). You have a gazillion Facebook friends. Think about all the people you could encourage!" His response was, "Maybe," which our daughter Emilie would say really means "No." But I couldn't get it out of my head. He NEEDED to do this, so I asked him again and that's when things got ugly. He was washing dishes and without looking up, said (with this little all-knowing, annoying smirk), "No. YOU should do it." I was frustrated. Here I was presenting him with this awesome opportunity and he was going to pass on it. Then he REALLY rubbed salt into the wound. "You said you wanted to write to help people. You even went back to school to get your degree in English. So write. Put your money where your mouth is. Maybe the reason you can't get this idea out of your head is because YOU'RE supposed to do it." I HATE it when he's right.

At first, it was just a few sentences attached to a verse, but over time I gained confidence and before I knew it I was writing stories. I made a decision to be transparent. I wanted people to know that no one has it all together and that they are not alone in their pain. Right away, I started getting feedback from people whom I hadn't talked to in over twenty years. I heard from friends who were going through some really difficult times and asking for prayer. I received texts from people who don't follow Jesus but could identify with my struggles and found my stories encouraging. "Please don't stop" they said, so I didn't. Easter came and went and I kept on writing. That is how *#littleseedsofhope* was born.

Who is this book for?

If you are someone who would not call yourself a Christian, but you are curious about Jesus and need encouragement, then this book is for you. If you are a burnt-out Christian whose heart has been broken and are tired of putting on the "My Life is Perfect" mask, then this book is for you. Maybe you've been friends with Jesus a long time but need a new perspective, to hear a fresh voice, then this book is for you as well.

How to use this book?

Think of this as 100 dates with God. I want this to be low pressure. If you want to read it every day that's great! If you want to read it twice a week, that's great too! I didn't write this to cause stress, frustration or guilt! My suggestion is to grab a cup of your favorite beverage, find a quiet spot, spend a few minutes reading and see what thoughts surface, maybe say a prayer. Friend, praying is just talking to God. If that's hard to wrap your mind around, then imagine you are sending Him a text.

Me: Hi

God: Hi

Me: I'm worried about all that I have to do today and I'm not sure how I'm going to get everything done, which makes me anxious which makes me less likely to get anything accomplished, which makes me more anxious....I need help. (grimace emoji, praying hands)

God: You got it! I'm sending you a Helper. Love you. (Thumbs up emoji, heart, muscle arm)

I've also included a song at the end of each encounter. Some are songs that I have enjoyed for a while and some are new songs that I love and were recommended by friends. I hope they enhance your time with God.

Why do I even need to spend time with God?

This is what time with God has done for me...

I have less anxiety and more JOY! I'm an anxious, over-thinker by nature. The more time I spend remembering how God has provided and come through for me in the past, the less anxious I feel about His ability to care for me in the future. As my anxiety has decreased, my capacity to enjoy today has exponentially improved.

God and I talk. I've remembered that He's my friend. My prayers are more personal, more other focused, full of gratitude and less about a list of things I want or need or need to be fixed.

I feel like a huge weight has been lifted off my shoulders. I'm no longer afraid to be real. Being a pastor's wife and worship leader doesn't mean I have to put a phony mask of perfection. I will NOT be ashamed of the places where God has rebuilt and restored my life. I am a work in progress. He is making me beautiful and He ALWAYS finishes what He starts.

Beloved, if you are reading this, know that I am praying for you. I'm praying that my stories of failure and redemption will fill you with hope and anticipation of what God can do in YOUR life. I am also praying that you will come to know that God is for you and He cares about your life, every part, even the small things. Basically, He's crazy about you, thinks you're awesome and wants to hang out and bless you. True story.

Love, *Maria*

Plant HOPE. Grow LOVE. Share FAITH.

#littleseedsofhope

DAY 1

I used to work with a woman who didn't like me. Something about me just crawled under her skin. I would say, "Good Morning", only to be met with silence. I decided that for her birthday I would pull out all the stops. I brought her a bouquet of flowers, a card and even made a birthday cake. Right before lunchtime she marched into my office and threw the flowers and card on my desk and essentially said to take my happiness and smiles and good mornings and put them where the sun doesn't shine because life was tough and I had no idea what she was going through. Then she stomped out of the room and slammed the door. I was speechless. What had just happened? I was just being nice! It took me several days of self-examination to come to the conclusion that I had been acting like a plastic person. Yes, I said good morning and smiled, but I never went any deeper. I had never asked her about her weekend, or how her day was going, or if there was anything I could do to help with her work load. I had no idea if she was married or had children. I never "saw" her. Humbled, I began to make tiny overtures towards real friendship. I think she felt bad for yelling at me, so she was friendlier too. We never became best friends but she told me about her boyfriend, that she was completely overwhelmed at work, and had recently lost fifty pounds! When I left that job, SHE actually gave ME a card! This is what I learned: Jesus cared about people on the deepest level. If I want to be like Him, kind words are not enough, I actually need to care too. Love and friendship are priceless gifts that can't be bought with plastic.

#kindwordsANDactions #blindbutnowIsee #lovePeopleloveJesus
#littleseedsofhope

Be kind and compassionate to one another, forgiving each other, just as in Christ God forgave you. Ephesians 4:32

Simple Gospel by United Pursuit

DAY 2

On a snowy New England day, I was waiting in the parking lot of our daughter Emilie's school, when a sudden movement under one of the cars caught my eye. What I thought was a big lump of icy snow began to move! Huddled and shivering was a large, grey domestic rabbit that someone had abandoned. With the help of another mom, I picked her up and carefully put her in a box. It became immediately obvious she was not well. I called a local vet who agreed to examine her for free. The poor bunny had such a severe case of mites that permanent damage had been caused to her ears. She had lost her sense of direction and would hop in circles and even flip over and over if she was agitated. "Annie", (after one of Emilie's favorite movies), was loved on by our family for about a year until she went to bunny heaven. Have you ever felt like my little orphaned bunny? Have you been hurt and abandoned by people whom you trusted and loved? Do you need to be rescued from going in emotional circles? Beloved, when I am feeling like this, I run to Jesus. He is my sanity, my refuge, my security, and to quote Princess Leia, "my only hope." People will fail me and I will fail them. It doesn't mean we should stop having relationships. It does means that we need to stop putting each other on pedestals and instead, elevate the ONLY ONE who can really save the day.

#myHero #FaithfulANDTrue #Deliverer #SetsUSfree #ourROCK
#PrinceofPeace #littleseedsofhope

You are my refuge and my shield; I have put my hope in your word.
Psalm 119:114

You Are Not Alone by Kari Jobe

DAY 3

My husband Foye and I were recently in Kentucky for a wedding and in our spare time we visited a nearby brewery/distillery. On the tour, the guide told us about beer fermented in barrels that used to hold bourbon. They said that after the bourbon is removed from the barrel an astounding one to two gallons remains soaked into the wood. This is called, "The Devil's Cut." When the barrels are then filled with beer, this leftover bourbon taints or flavors it, however you'd like to look at it. I found this fascinating and said to Foye, "Wow! People are just like barrels." Friend, since then I've been thinking about my own "Devil's Cut." Over the years, I have allowed a lot of things to saturate my life and now I struggle with the consequences of some of those choices. I found this thought really discouraging, but then I did a little research and found that barrels can be washed! If soaked in a special water solution, over time you can leach out The Devil's Cut. Friend, Jesus offers us this special water solution for free! When we spend time with Him by reading the Bible, praying or listening to worship music, we are soaked in this beautiful, refreshing, "Living Water" and The Devil's Cut is leached out of our hearts and lives. It's a slow process, and at first it may seem like nothing is happening but don't give up! Change WILL happen, my life is proof. Beloved, our barrels won't be fully restored until the day we join Jesus in Heaven, but until then life can smell and taste so much sweeter.

*#thirstyforJesus #wateroflife #neverrunsdry #HemakesALLthingsNEW
#RESTORED #littleseedsofhope*

*... to make her holy, cleansing her by the washing with water
through the word, Ephesians 5:26*

In Christ Alone by Passion

DAY 4

Recently, I watched two people who struggle with food addiction fall off the wagon. Both had been having great success and then stress bombs were dropped in their lives. Instead of turning to Jesus, they turned to binge eating. Both times I tried to intervene by reminding them of how great they had been doing and the consequences of their actions. Both times I was turned away, once with anger and once with humor, but the message was the same, "Mind your own business. I need this right now. I can't deal with my addiction and this stressful situation." It was hard to watch because I love these people. It was hard to watch because I saw and heard MYSELF. I once had a doctor say, "The only way to get rid of an addiction is to replace it with something good, something healthy. If you don't, another (soul sucking) addiction will take its place and you will find yourself worse off than you were before." Friend, when stressful situations come, I want to choose Jesus. I want to crawl up into His lap instead of crawling into a refrigerator. It seems to me that a soldier's main job is to train. They prepare and practice so that when the enemy attacks they are ready to fight and defend their ground. I am training too but not to fight. I am learning to run. I am not a coward, but this enemy feels bigger than I am. So, my plan is to RUN as fast and hard as I can, straight to Jesus. I am going to let Him fight temptation for me because victory tastes better than chocolate. It's true! Beloved, will you run with me today?

#soldierintraining #faithnotfood #gogogo #byebyebadchoice #JesusStrong #littleseedsofhope

Cast your cares on the LORD and he will sustain you; Psalm 55:22

Lose My Soul by Toby Mac

DAY 5

Some of you know that my husband Foye is a Prayer Warrior and a Firefighter. This was not always the case. When Foye and I were dating, he confided that he felt far away from God. This may be hard to imagine, but back then he wouldn't pray and he didn't like people. Foye was hurting because leaders at the church where he grew up had made poor choices and as a young man in the Marines, he hadn't always obeyed Jesus either. He felt unworthy of God's love AND angry at how badly God's people sometimes treated each other. At that time, our romance was long distance. Foye lived in Connecticut and I lived in Pennsylvania. This was before cell phones, so we wrote LETTERS to each other every day. I'm a romantic, and wrote my letters on pink scented paper (you may laugh), and I would add a Bible verse to remind him of Jesus' passionate and unconditional LOVE. The verse below was one that I sent. Beloved, there is no doubt in this life we will walk through fire. However, Jesus calls us to do more than just endure the flames. He wants us to be like a fireman with all of our turnout gear on. The Bible calls this putting on The Armor of God. More importantly, Jesus is calling us to fight for each other in His name. Beloved, have you put on your armor? The battle is REAL! The fire is HOT! Firefighter Foye is going to battle for the sake of God's people, every day! Will you join him in kicking Satan's @&$!!

#walkthroughfire #PUTonYOURarmor #warriorpriest #littleseedsofhope

When you pass through the waters, I will be with you; and when you pass through the rivers, they will not sweep over you.
When you walk through the fire, you will not be burned; the flames will not set you ablaze. Isaiah 43:2

Champion by Brian and Katie Torwalt

DAY 6

When I heard that one of my favorite designers, Kate Spade, committed suicide my heart broke for her family. If you wonder how someone could do that to the people they love, I will tell you. Several years ago I considered suicide but decided I didn't really want to die, just disappear. I even thought about how much money I would need to make it happen, to run away from my life. I was super busy at church, at work and at home. BUT, I was not spending time with Jesus or taking care of myself. As a result, I felt increasingly overwhelmed and depressed. The word FAILURE was on a continuous loop in my head. I was convinced that my husband and children would be better off without me. Foye could remarry someone who wasn't fat, and who also was smarter, more spiritual, nicer, happier, a better mother...etc., etc. Beloved, Jesus used a friend to expose all the lies I was believing. He opened the door for counseling and I made a decision to be ruthlessly transparent about my insecurities. I never want to be trapped in my own head again. Why am I sharing this? Because I think that there might be someone out there who feels like I did, who needs a friend to dispel the lies. If that's you, please listen, YOU ARE LOVED. You are NOT alone. You are very, VERY precious to Papa God. Your life matters! PLEASE, get out of your head. Tell someone TODAY that you need help.

#HOPEisREAL #dontbelievethelies #youareneeded #jesuslovesyou #precious #littleseedsofhope

But the eyes of the Lord are on those who fear him, on those whose hope is in his unfailing love, Psalm 33:18

Break Every Chain by Jesus Culture

DAY 7

The first year Foye and I were married was sometimes wonderful and mostly NOT. I remember calling up my mother and saying, "Mom, I think I've made a mistake." Part of the problem was that I made a big deal out of EVERYTHING and Foye was ultra-laid back. He accurately described me as pugnacious. I was gripped by terrible fear and anxiety that we would end up divorced like my parents. We had to fix things, immediately! I misunderstood the saying, "Don't let the sun go down on your anger." While it's not good to hold onto hard feelings from one day to the next, I thought it also meant that everything needed to be completely resolved before we went to bed. As I've grown older and hopefully wiser, I've learned that relationships take lots of work and time. We can't fix each other. We can share our hearts and concerns, but ultimately we have to get on our knees, pray and give things to Jesus for Him to sort out. Some people say that fear is a great motivator. While that may be true, what it motivates us to do is often not helpful. Love is a much, MUCH better motivator. Remember, "Love is patient and kind, not envious or boastful, arrogant or rude, doesn't insist on its own way, isn't irritable, resentful, or joyous when evil wins. Love rejoices with the truth, bears all things, believes all things, hopes all things, endures all things. Love never fails!"

#chooselove #forgive #olderandwiser #littleseedsofhope

For I am the Lord your God who takes hold of your right hand and says to you, Do not fear; I will help you. Isaiah 41:13

How He Loves by David Crowder Band

DAY 8

I was praying with my friend Chad when a startling image came to my mind. "Chad!" I said, "I think God wants you to be The Naked Guy!" The Naked Guy is a man who walks around a town in NY, where we used to live, collecting recycling. He's barefoot, wears only a pair of shorts, even in the winter. I thought he was homeless until one day The Naked Guy showed up at our church and we learned his story. He walks barefoot to be close to the earth. He wears little clothes to reject consumerism, and gives all the money from the recycling to the poor. He WANTS people to ask questions so that he can share the Gospel. Foye calls him a modern day Ascetic, like St. Francis. Chad looked at me with surprise and said, "I never wear shorts because of the scars on my leg. People always ask questions." Friends, Chad has an amazing story. Not long ago he was literally dying in a hospital, in the grip of addiction and getting ready to have his leg amputated. A stranger walked into the room, prayed with him and next morning his leg and body were miraculously healed. "Chad," I said, "you NEED to wear shorts so you can tell people your story!" I think Chad's scars are BEAUTIFUL! They are marks of the great and miraculous love that Jesus has for him. I have to tell you, when Chad came over our house the other day, one of the first things out of his mouth was, "Hey Maria, I've been wearing shorts!" Beloved, do you have scars that you are hiding?

#nakedforJesus #letyourlightshine #beautifulscars #littleseedsofhope

I will also make you a light for the Gentiles, that my salvation may reach to the ends of the earth. Isaiah 49:6

Less Like Scars by Sara Groves

DAY 9

Watching Prince Harry marry a girl of mixed race made me cry. You may not think of me as of mixed race but growing up on Long Island in the 1970's, I was definitely considered "other." In kindergarten, I had to be the first one off the school bus and the last one on for my safety. The other children would throw garbage and call me racial slurs. So in elementary school, I made it my mission to prove that I was not only just like everyone else but smarter! The world has changed, but still almost 80 percent of the people I meet ask me about my ethnicity. In all honesty, it feels like I'm being sorted so people know what little box they can put me in. However, now my mission has changed. I no longer have anything to prove. I no longer need to be the smartest person in the room. Now, I want to be the kindest. I want to show ALL people the love of Jesus, even if I never say His name during one of our conversations. I feel like a secret agent, sowing seeds of kindness and love in unexpected places. Each day, I pray that people will ask me, "Why?" and I will be given the opportunity to share about the ONE who is my source of ALL my strength, joy and ANY kindness that I have within me.

#iamaprincesstoo #myDaddyistheKingofKings #secretagent #sowkindness
#littleseedsofhope

Do not be deceived: God cannot be mocked.
A man reaps what he sows. Galatians 6:7

King of My Heart by Bethel Music

DAY 10

Jesus was kind to women. He loved on them, listened to them, taught them, healed them...they were his friends. Women, however, are not always as kind to one another. I remember Emilie noticing this in high school. "Mom, why don't girls give each other compliments? I never hear anyone say, "Your hair looks nice today, or great job on that test. All I hear is people tearing each other down." So Emilie made it her mission to give a compliment to EVERY woman/girl she met ALL DAY, EVERY DAY. It didn't matter if it was the lady at the checkout line in Walmart or a girl in her Chemistry class, she always found something nice to say. She would tell me that people looked shocked and didn't know what to do. Sometimes, so unused to compliments, women thought she was poking fun, so she had to reassure them of her sincerity. I realized that society trains our girls to be in constant competition with one another. Jesus, on the other hand tells us that the church is one body, one team. Watching my girl change the world of those around her with kind words made me see my own critical and judgmental spirit. So, I joined Emilie on her mission. It is one of my proudest moments as a mom. Will you join us on this mission today too?

#planthope #growlove#sharefaith #Emiliesmission #littleseedsofhope

Charm is deceptive, and beauty is fleeting; but a woman who fears the Lord is to be praised. Proverbs 31:30

By Our Love by Christy Nockles

DAY II

Our son Zayden has been watching *The Lord of the Rings*. He loves that the fate of the world rests upon the shoulders of one little hobbit. (He's a "root for the underdog" kind of kid). Zayden is VERY concerned that Frodo is going to give in to temptation and lose everything. He gets all worked up and emotionally involved, forgetting that it's just a movie. I've had to reassure him several times, to have faith, that everything will work out in the end. I know this with certainty because I've already watched the movies AND read the book. The look he gives me is skeptical. This is because at eleven years old, Zayden knows temptation is very, very powerful. He struggles with it every day just like his parents. It's much easier to believe that bad things will happen than to have faith in an ending that seems to defy all the odds. Sometimes just like my little man, I need faith to believe that Jesus is a real person and not just a fictional hero in a story of love and sacrifice. I need faith to believe He's coming back someday to undo all the wrong and make all things new. The Bible says to ask for faith and God PROMISES to give it to you. It doesn't have to be a fancy prayer either, just say, "God help me to believe!" or "God I need some faith!" Beloved, will you pray with me today?

#faithplease #LOTRfamily #teamhobbit #teamjesus

And without faith it is impossible to please God, because anyone who comes to him must believe that he exists and that he rewards those who earnestly seek him. Hebrews 11:6

Jesus I Believe by Big Daddy Weave

DAY 12

We were in the middle of trying to adopt Zayden when our lawyer called and said, "I think you should give up. Rhode Island Department of Social Services is not going to let this child go out of state. I can continue to take your money but you're not going to win." I was devastated and after telling Foye, went into the kitchen and cried ugly, angry tears, banging around pots and pans and slamming cabinets as I attempted to make some sort of dinner. At the time Emilie was only twelve years old (going on forty. That child was born old). She walked into the kitchen and said with strange authority, "Mom, you have been trying so hard to make this happen on your own strength. I don't think that's how God works. If Zayden is meant to be part of our family it will happen. If you believe that, why are you so upset?" The words were an arrow of conviction straight to my heart. God had spoken directly to me through my child. That night, Foye and I made a decision to throw in the towel and early the next day he made the call to our lawyer. Beloved, that's when, thanks to the wisdom of a twelve year old, I got to see Papa God move in a mighty and miraculous way. You know how the story ends. In July 2018, we celebrated Zayden's ninth Gotcha Day. Woot! Woot!! God is GOOD!

#hecanmovemountains #jesusibelieve #outofthemouthofbabes
#preacherskid #littleseedsofhope

Don't let anyone look down on you because you are young,
but set an example for the believers in speech, in conduct, in love,
in faith and in purity. 1 Timothy 4:12

My Story by Big Daddy Weave

DAY 13

My brother Joe makes AMAZING pizza. He knows where to the find the freshest mozzarella cheese, how to make homemade, deliciously thick marinara sauce and of course, craft the perfect crust. He can even toss it up in the air with just a flick of his wrist. I once asked him, "Am I imagining things or does NY City pizza taste better?" He said it's all about the water. NY City water comes from the Catskill Mountains. It has a unique mineral content that when mixed with the flour and yeast, makes dough that lightly crusts on the outside while remaining soft and fluffy on the inside. Ideal for cutting into slices that easily fold into little hand-held pieces of heaven. Are you hungry yet? We also talked about imposter pizza. It looks like pizza, it smells like pizza but it's NOT! The mozzarella is replaced by a cheese-like product, the crust is too chewy or too dry and tastes... meh. Whenever I've settled for an imposter or a cheap imitation, I've walked away feeling dissatisfied and frustrated. Beloved, are you hungry for the real deal? Do you want food that always satisfies the longings of your soul? Let me tell you about The Bread of Life. It's unlike ANYTHING you've ever eaten and even has healing properties. Do you want some of this heavenly bread? Don't worry I'm connected. I can hook you up with my guy J.C. True story, before He got into the food industry He used to be a carpenter.

#breadoflife #neverhungryagain #sliceofheaven #igottaguy
#littleseedsofhope

Then Jesus declared, "I am the bread of life. Whoever comes to me will never go hungry, and whoever believes in me will never be thirsty."
John 6:35

Revelation Song by Kari Jobe

DAY 14

I have inadvertently become a connoisseur of gas station cuisine. It wasn't a life goal, but I'm often in a rush, I don't pack my lunch and by 1 o'clock I'm scrounging around my car looking for gum, a mint, anything to eat. So I stop at a gas station and buy one of those *taquito* things or some other barely recognizable non organic, GMO laden food-like product. Fifteen minutes later I'm full but my stomach hurts and I feel awful for the rest of the day. I can't even complain to Foye because he offers to make me lunch ALL THE TIME. If roles were reversed and he was eating stuff that made him sick I would be all over him about not taking care of himself, not planning ahead, and wasting money. Hypocritical, I know. So I hide the evidence in the garage trash can as soon as I get home. They say insanity is doing the same thing over and over but expecting different results. Guilty. I'm outing myself because this verse convicted me. Why do I settle for trashy mystery meat when I have a fridge full of delicious Greek yogurt, lettuce wraps, AND a lovely husband who's willing to pack it all up in my cute Vera Bradley lunch sack? Why do I rebel against planning ahead? I've been thinking about this verse for a couple of weeks and praying, "Jesus show me the areas in my life where am I settling for the bitter." Beloved, this is not just about crappy food. There are times when my heart, my soul is starving and I've fed it garbage as well. It only takes five minutes for Foye to make me lunch. It only takes five minutes to start your day with a verse and a prayer. It's a tiny commitment in the big scheme of things. Friend, will you choose to be healthy with me? I want the sweet in ALL of my life. Today, let's chose the honey and take out the trash.

#sweetlife #saynotomysterymeat #5minutestowinit #yeswecan
#littleseedsofhope

One who is full loathes honey from the comb, but to the hungry even what is bitter tastes sweet. Proverbs 27:7

The More I Seek You by Kari Jobe

DAY 15

In May of 2005, my friend Heather and I went to South Africa for a nursing symposium on HIV and Tuberculosis. One of the places we would visit was an orphanage and the organizers of the trip distributed a list of items that the children needed. Heather knew a dentist who gladly donated a bunch of little toothbrushes and toothpastes that we carefully packed in our luggage. When we got to customs, the official (with a gun strapped to his back) tried to make us pay a "tax" on the items, somewhere between 30 and 50 dollars. I became livid, unleashed my Sicilian temper and said, "No! I am not paying a tax. Go find your supervisor. I am trying to help the children of YOUR country and you are NOT going to tax me for it!" Looking back I am not sure if I was fearless or foolish. Beloved, anger can cause a lot of damage. When my emotions are high it's harder to control what comes out of my mouth. In this situation I was lucky the guard didn't throw me in a foreign jail or worse over toothbrushes with little characters on them. I was meditating this morning on what makes me angry. I confess that one of those things is my son. It's very hard for me not take it personally when he is naughty, especially when I've told him one thousand times not to do something. However, this is after Foye has reminded ME one thousand times that Zayden is just being foolish and has little impulse control. The Bible says that Father God is slow to anger and overflowing with love. I don't think that's how Zayden would describe his mom right now. Beloved, today is a new day and I really want to be a better version of myself. Do you? This is my prayer and it can be yours too, "Jesus, I'm sorry. I'm laying MY foolishness down at Your feet. I know You are good at making broken things new. Please change my heart, and make me more like You."

#lifegoals#slowtoanger #aboundinginlove #fullofgraceandmercy
#littleseedsofhope

Do not be quickly provoked in your spirit,
for anger resides in the lap of fools. Ecclesiastes 7:9

Mended by Matthew West

DAY 16

My junior year of college was a wonderful year because I met my future husband AND I learned what it means to have a sister. I ALWAYS wanted to have a sister and Papa God sent me a roommate named Tiffany. I remember the first time she offered to share clothes. It may sound silly but I wanted to cry. I hadn't even known her very long, but she didn't hold back. She was warm, kind, and generous right from the get-go. That year she even invited me to go on vacation with her family. Tiffany made an enormous impression on my life. This verse reminded me that Jesus is my big brother and just like Tiffany, He shares his clothes with me. Jesus' clothes are so cool, so incredible, they have names like "The Robes of Righteousness" and they are made by The Designer...of the universe. But this is where things get a little weird. He won't let me wear His clothes unless I give Him my dirty old rags SO HE CAN WEAR THEM! I'm like, "Jesus, this stuff is gross, stained (with sin), and really, really nasty. I'm totally embarrassed to even show it to you." And He's like, "Hand it over. It's only way you can wear My stuff." So I did it. I gave Jesus my disgusting, sin stained, smelly clothes and Beloved, You can too!!! Oh and this is THE BEST PART! He will never ask you for His cool clothes back. NEVER. They're yours to keep FOREVER!

#number1brother #GreatestOfAllTime #familyforever #madeinheaven #littleseedsofhope

God made him who had no sin to be sin for us, so that in him we might become the righteousness of God. 2 Corinthians 5:21

Garment of Praise by Robin Mark

DAY 17

I was meditating on this verse and praying about what to write and an image came to my mind. Foye and I were two oak trees planted right next to a river. We were tall, straight and strong because our roots went deep and we drank of the sweet river water all day and all night. In front of the trees was a bench where children were playing, running around laughing and enjoying the cool shade. I knew that these were our children and grandchildren. Then couples came to sit on the bench, holding hands and talking with heads bent close. These were the young men and young women whom we have mentored and loved upon over the years. I said to the Lord, "This is beautiful but I don't understand what this has to do with Psalm 1 verses 1 and 2", and Papa said, "Keep reading." So I pulled up Psalm 1 on my phone and verse 3 says… "And he shall be like a tree planted by the rivers of water, that bringeth forth his fruit in his season; his leaf also shall not wither; and whatsoever he doeth shall prosper." Beloved, I am weepy with gratitude. The only reason I am planted by the river is because the Master Gardener picked me when I was just a sapling and transplanted me to His garden. Friend, is your soul tired and thirsty today? Do you need to drink from the river that NEVER runs dry? There's plenty of room in Papa God's garden and I would LOVE it if you asked Him to plant you right next to me.

#rootedinHim #cometotheriver #livinglegacy #grateful #family
#littleseedsofhope

Blessed is the one who does not walk in step with the wicked or stand in the way that sinners take or sit in the company of mockers,
Psalm 1:1

My Simple Prayer by Maria Belyea

DAY 18

Emilie loves *Harry Potter* and our dog Luna is named after a character in one of the books. A couple of years ago she called me from college full of excitement! "Mom! There is a town outside of Philly that holds a Harry Potter festival and I really want to go!! Will you come with me?" Of course I said, "Yes!" Anytime my girl wants to hang out with her Momma, the answer is always, "Yes!" The day arrived and I picked Emilie up at the airport. Parking was terrible! We had to park at least a mile and a half from the festival. It was really cold and rainy, but Emilie and thousands of other Potter Heads didn't care. They were in Harry Potter heaven! Despite the rain, we had a wonderful time. This morning I was thinking about what devotion to Jesus is supposed to look like and our Harry Potter adventure came to mind. I thought about all the people in costume, who on a normal day look like everyone else unless you looked closely and noticed they have a Harry Potter tattoo, or a mug on their desk that says, "Slytherin", or a cat named Hermione. Harry Potter Day gave them a chance to outwardly revel in their obsession, to let all their Harry Potter love free! Beloved, I want to love Jesus like those folks love Harry Potter. When I meet other Christians I want to be like, "Yassssss!!! Me tooo!!! Jesus is my favorite!! I'm obsessed with Jesus!! I've read His books like a million times, I've totally memorized the second book! Want to come over and have a praise and worship marathon?"

#changemyheartohGod #makeitevertrue #devotion #Jesusfangirl
#littleseedsofhope

Keep this Book of the Law always on your lips; meditate on it day and night, so that you may be careful to do everything written in it. Then you will be prosperous and successful. Joshua 1:8

Lord I Need You by Matt Maher

DAY 19

At the very first church we served, a woman named Maria opened her heart and home to us and loved Emilie like a granddaughter. Every Friday night, Maria would have her grandchildren come for a sleepover and Emilie was included in festivities. When we first moved to NY, I had to stay behind for a few months and was going to miss Emilie's 11th birthday. I was devastated. A kind woman named Marianne threw her a lovely birthday party and took her kayaking for the first time. Over the years there have been times when Foye and I were struggling financially and someone from church paid our rent or bought groceries. It wasn't just because Foye was the pastor either. I've watched churchy people do all kinds of extraordinary, selfless acts of kindness and love for each other. Why? It's because of "Ohana", to quote Lilo and Stitch. We are an enormous, messy, wonderful, and terrible family. Frequently we emphasize the terrible, and when family hurts you it's the worst kind of pain. We ALSO need to talk about the blessings, the comfort, and the small sacrifices that happen every day! If we want more people to get adopted into this crazy Jesus Ohana, we need to share why this family is AWESOME! We also need to BE the kind of family member that people want to be around. It's a new day, let's start it right! Take out those pictures like a proud granny and brag to someone about your Jesus Ohana. If you are just checking this Jesus thing out, come on over! Mangia! Eat with us! There's always room for one more at the family table!

#jesusismybigbrother #lovemyfamily #mangia #familyforever #ohana #littleseedsofhope

But you are a chosen people, a royal priesthood, a holy nation, God's special possession, that you may declare the praises of him who called you out of darkness into his wonderful light. 1 Peter 2:9

Who You Say I Am by Hillsong

DAY 20

When Zayden was in preschool we went on a short hike to Auger Falls. It's a flat walk and only a half-mile each way. Foye encouraged Zayden to walk on his own but he tripped over every root, kept on trying to run off the path and fell multiple times in the bushes and mud. He whined, complained and Foye ended up carrying him. When we arrived at the falls, amazed by their beauty and noise, Zayden laughed with glee and made a beeline for the drop off. I think Jesus sent children into my life to help me understand His great love and endless patience for me! It doesn't matter how many times Foye has to pick Zayden up, dust him off and rescue him from danger, he LOVES THAT BOY! He is Foye's JOY and the feelings are mutual. Zayden, now eleven years old, sticks to Foye closer than a burr lodged in Luna's fur. It's ALL about his Daddy. I'm ok with that. It's beautiful to watch. Beloved, to "abide" is a fancy way of saying to make a person your home. I can say with confidence that Foye is definitely Zayden's person, his home. Friend, do you need a place to abide? Are you looking for a home for your heart? You are in luck because I know of an open house! Don't worry, the owner is a friend. He's also a carpenter and does REALLY good work.

#welcomehome #stuckonyouJesus #littleseedsofhope

I am the vine; you are the branches. If you remain in me and I in you, you will bear much fruit; apart from me you can do nothing. John 15:5

He's Always Been Faithful by Sara Groves

DAY 21

I used to have this romanticized ideal that to really serve Jesus I had to go to a different country. I imagined myself in Africa, only I would look like Angelina Jolie, delicately sweating while I balanced a child on my hip as I saved the world. I prayed that Jesus would send me to some exotic place, but the years passed and I never realized my dream. Then one day, I walked into the clinic where I worked in Albany, NY and it hit me. I didn't need to go to Africa to be a missionary, Papa God had brought the mission field to me. I looked around the room and saw patients from China, Russia, Afghanistan and Southeast Asia. They were refugees who had come to the US for asylum. I thought of the rack of clothing and shoes we collected and handed out weekly to people in need. I remembered the stash of food I kept in my office for children who were hungry. I was living Matthew 35:35-36 at work! "For I was hungry and you gave me something to eat, I was thirsty and you gave me something to drink, I was a stranger and you invited me in, I needed clothes and you clothed me, I was sick and you looked after me." Excited by this revelation, I ran into my office to call Foye. He laughed and teased me that Jesus knew I wouldn't have lasted long living in a hut with giant bugs and no air conditioning. Beloved, that day I realized that just because I couldn't openly talk about Jesus at work didn't mean I couldn't BE Jesus at work, AND if I am not trying to be like Jesus, no one really wants to hear what I have to say anyway.

#loveJESUSlovePEOPLE #bethehandsandfeetHERE #sowlove #growfaith
#littleseedsofhope

walk in the way of love, just as Christ loved us and gave himself up for us as a fragrant offering and sacrifice to God. Ephesians 5:2

I Will Follow by Chris Tomlin

DAY 22

Foye was teaching Jr. High at North Stonington Christian Academy and asked me to help his class with their part in the Christmas program. To free my hands, the preschool teacher invited Emilie, who was only two, to hang out with her class. That night the sweetest little sounds of Emilie singing could be heard in our home. The preschoolers had also been practicing for Christmas and Emilie had learned all four verses of "Away in a Manger." "Emilie", I asked, "Will you sing that for the people at Church?" Without missing a beat she looked at me and said, "I need a ballerina dress with a poofy skirt." I immediately bought one and she sang during our Wednesday night service without fear and completely confident that she was loved and accepted. One of my first times singing in church did not go as well. I messed up, stopped singing, had a panic attack, and ran off stage to hide in the nursery. I was so embarrassed and fearful of what people might think. Fortunately, the choir director found me. I don't remember exactly what she said but here's what I got out of our talk: I am loved. Everyone makes mistakes and has embarrassing moments. We sing for an audience of One and Jesus is more concerned with the condition of my heart than whether or not I hit the right note. That day I didn't fall down, I fell forward. I messed up but grew in faith, fear lost a little of its grip on me and I took my first baby steps towards becoming a Worship Leader for hundreds of people. Beloved, what fears (lies) are stopping you from becoming the person you were created to be?

#fallforward #lovedANDaccepted #audienceofone #fearisaliar
#littleseedsofhope

For the Spirit God gave us does not make us timid, but gives us power, love and self-discipline. 2 Timothy 1:7

Fierce by Jesus Culture

DAY 23

At Zayden's age, I was so awkward and terrible at sports that I was placed in remedial gym class. Twice a week during recess, our motley crew of mostly nerdy misfits, had to run laps around the gym and then do push-ups and sit ups. It was someone's brilliant idea that this would improve our Presidential Physical Fitness scores. It was an abysmal failure. Imagine half a dozen, whining children limping around the gymnasium, slower than molasses. I still have the occasional nightmare about it. Although Zayden is not my biological child, he has somehow inherited my lack of athletic ability. It's not that he doesn't want to participate. It's just so much easier to quit when it seems like everyone else is running circles around you. I've been thinking about how to help my son, particularly as he goes to Junior High next year. Although some people have natural ability, most of us can significantly improve if we practice. In fact, repetition reprograms your brain and eventually, you develop neural pathways or "grooves." My little man needs his family to help him get into "the groove" with some physical training, or as Foye says, "PT." Friend, are you feeling like you are in remedial Jesus class? Does it seem like faith comes so easily for others. Please don't give up. You just need a little "ST" or Spiritual Training. Start out like I did with committing the first few minutes each day to Jesus. Find an app that will send you a daily Bible verse. Read it. Spend a minute or two thinking about what it means and a minute or two praying, which is literally just talking to Jesus. Tell Him what you are thankful for and what worries you and watch as your spiritual muscles grow! Warning: you may find yourself wearing tank tops and flexing those beauties all over the place. Just sayin'.

#getintotheJesusgroove #ImgonnapumpYOUup #practicemakespermanent #SpiritualTraining #littleseedsofhope

With God we will gain the victory, and he will trample down our enemies.
Psalm 60:12

Run by Paul Coleman

DAY 24

I am a visiting nurse and the majority of my patients are elderly. It is not uncommon for me to enter a home where the television is blaring (because my patients are hard of hearing), and nine times out of ten, they are watching the news. The conversation frequently starts like this,

> Me- "Hi my name is Maria."
>
> Mrs. X - "What?"
>
> Me - "My name is Maria."
>
> Mrs. X - "Can you repeat that?"
>
> Me - "I'm Maria your nurse."
>
> Mrs. X - "I'm sorry I can't understand you."
>
> Me - "Do you mind if we turn down the TV?"

Regardless of who they voted for, the news upsets them, and yet they can't seem to turn it off. All day long the talking heads make them anxious, raise their blood pressure and even cause despair. I've had many unfruitful discussions about alternatives like watching a classic movie on Netflix, or listening to a book on tape. The best I've been able to accomplish is turning down the volume while I am providing their care. There are many circumstances in life that are outside of our control. However, we have choices about what we feed our minds. I'm not saying don't watch the news, but watching my patients suffer has made me evaluate what I dwell on and obsess over. It's pretty clear that if I want the peace of Jesus then I have to spend time with Him. Beloved, I want and need more peace, don't you? Will you turn down the noise and tune up the JOY with me?

#pray #readthebible #getyourworshipon #recipeforpeace #littleseedsofhope

Peace I leave with you; my peace I give you. I do not give to you as the world gives. Do not let your hearts be troubled and do not be afraid.
John 14:27

Tremble by Mosaic

DAY 25

I once housesat for someone whose home was infested with roach-es. During the first few days I saw an occasional straggler. I was in denial and convinced myself it was an aberration. Have I mentioned that I really, really, REALLY HATE bugs? Then one night I woke up and needed to use the bathroom. Y'all know where this is going. I turned on the bathroom light to wash my hands and THERE THEY WERE! For a moment we both stood frozen in the blinding fluores-cent light. I'm not ashamed to say I ran out of the room screaming as they scrambled frantically back to their hiding places. The next day I decided that one of us had to go, so I declared war on the dis-gusting roaches. This is where my husband would make a joke and say, "Roaches need love too." NO! No they DON'T!!! Sin has a lot in common with roaches. It likes to hide and we like to pretend it's not even there. Jesus, however, is called the Light of the World. His truth exposes every nasty sin, not to condemn us, but to show us where we need to clean house. Jesus loves us and wants us to be truly free from every sin that entangles us. I am not a gardener, but I do know that one small weed unattended will eventually choke out a garden. Sin ignored will choke out our joy, our faith and eventually destroy our witness for Christ. We have to be ruthless against our sin if we want to live the abundant and awesome life Papa has for us. (Side note: Beloved, please take care of your own roach problem before you start pestering a friend about theirs.) Are you ready? It's time. Turn on THE Light!

#cleanhouse #exterminateSIN #androaches #makeroomforJOY
#littleseedsofhope

Everyone who does evil hates the light, and will not come into the light for fear that their deeds will be exposed. John 3:20

Born Again by Austin French

DAY 26

Years ago I went on an African Safari in the famous Krueger National Park. The preserve we stayed at was called Tshukudu and specialized in rescuing lions. One day we were invited on a hike with a young lion. The guide explained that lions cannot be domesticated because once they turn a year old their hunting instincts kick in. This particular lion was not quite a year old and our guide told us to walk closely together. No one should appear "weak and slow" or the animal might pounce. Immediately, we closed ranks and began to walk as one entity with many legs. It was probably humorous to watch. Our translator was completely terrified because she was from a village where lions had killed several people. Quickly, we moved her to the safety of the center of the group and several of the women put their arms around her while murmuring words of reassurance. I've often thought of that day, when several dozen people walked in completely unity, huddled around the frightened and weak and thought, "That is how the church should look." If the strong gathered around the weak with the love and empathy of Jesus, then Satan would have no opportunity to devour anyone and our churches would be bursting at the seams.

#lovelikeJesus #onebody#family #gotyourback #nooneleftbehind
#littleseedofhope

Be alert and of sober mind. Your enemy the devil prowls around like a roaring lion looking for someone to devour. 1 Peter 5:8

Run Devil Run by Crowder

DAY 27

When I think of earthly sacrifice I think of my dad. Growing up we had one car. Dad would leave it at home for my mom and take the train to work instead. We lived over five miles away from the Hicksville station. Every day, Dad walked about a mile and then rode a bus to get there. Sometimes he worked very late and the busses weren't running, so he'd have to walk the whole way home. Rain or shine, snow or sleet, my dad faithfully went to work for his family. One year my mom splurged and bought him a beautiful parka. It had a fur hood and he looked like an Eskimo. My dad LOVED that coat. It wasn't very long afterwards that someone stole it. I was so upset. I cried and cried thinking about my daddy walking home in the cold without his Eskimo coat. He comforted me saying that maybe the person who stole it needed it more than he did. My father did not know that his loving sacrifice would help my faith. He gave me a small window into Papa God's heart as he modeled the phrase, "You sacrifice for the ones you love." Beloved, God didn't just offer a sacrifice for His children. He BECAME a human being because He loves you and me with an indescribable, never ending, unstoppable kind of love. That kind of love might be hard to wrap your mind around but it's the truth! Papa God is AWESOME like that!

#sacrifice #nogreaterlove#allforjoy #littleseedsofhope

He is the atoning sacrifice for our sins, and not only for ours but also for the sins of the whole world. 1 John 2:2

Above All by Michael W. Smith

DAY 28

Anyone who hears me speak and lead worship at church would probably never guess that I used to suffer from social anxiety and still do to a much smaller extent. Foye and I would attend a party or church function and I would need at least thirty minutes afterwards to "debrief." I'd go over every conversation, looking for mistakes or stupid things I may have said. Foye was super patient and reassuring that our friends were not perseverating on my every word. He also encouraged me to call someone if I thought I may have inadvertently offended them. So I did, and most of the time people didn't even remember the conversation. I was worried about nothing. Little by little I've come to realize that we ALL say things we regret. But we can't live in fear of making mistakes or we will isolate ourselves and miss out on life! I also can't control how people react. My true friends will love me even if I'm not perfect. Beloved, Papa God loves us better than any friends. He already knows every crazy thing you've ever said or will say, and He STILL loves you, LOVES you, LOVES YOU to the moon and back! Bring your hurts and failures to Him so He can ease your heart. His JOY is to make broken things new!

#makemeNEW #nofear#throneofGRACE
#HEdelightsinME #littleseedsofhope

Let us then approach God's throne of grace with confidence, so that
we may receive mercy and find grace to help us in our time of need.
Hebrews 4:16

Broken Things by Matthew West

DAY 29

My parents separated at the end of my freshman year of college. I was so angry with my father and wrongly blamed him for EVERYTHING. Two years later, I was at a Steven Curtis Chapman Concert and he spoke about the healing power of forgiveness. I realized that I needed and wanted to forgive my dad. After the concert, I waited on a long line to meet Steven. When it was my turn I asked if he would pray for me. Steven and his team huddled around and gently laid hands on me as they prayed for healing and restoration. It felt like a physical weight had been lifted off my shoulders. That night, I called my dad and told him that I forgave and loved him. We were still estranged, but it was a new beginning. As a parent, I have made many mistakes and realize that my dad was hurting and did the best he could with what he knew. Today, I look at him and see beauty in the brokenness because I know that the only perfect father is Papa God. Papa's beautiful, passionate, selfless, unrelenting love will never fail and I look forward to the day when I can say thank you, face to face. Happy Father's Day to my earthly Daddy and my Heavenly Daddy. I am so thankful for you both.

#papalovesme #daddysgirl #littleseedsofhope

A father to the fatherless, a defender of widows,
is God in his holy dwelling. Psalm 68:5

Mighty To Save by Laura Story

DAY 30

Several years back, I had a falling out with a close friend. I inadvertently hurt her feelings and she did not want to talk to me. We were both broken-hearted over the situation. I felt helpless so I did the only thing I could do, pray. I spent a lot of time in the ensuing months sitting on my little porch and journaling to God, asking Him to intervene on my behalf. For several agonizing months there was silence and then a tiny miracle happened. The friend reached out to ME, and little by little our friendship was restored. During that period of my life, as I spent a lot of time in introspection and examining my own heart, I thought about situations where I had denied someone forgiveness because I felt like their apology wasn't sincere. I learned a valuable lesson about not taking offense where none is intended. I also became thankful that neither Foye or Papa God are grudge holders. Friend, if you have given your life to Jesus, the cross works like an amazingly awesome, heavenly Instagram filter. When God sees you through it, ALL of your sins, past and future are GONE. Bye-bye. Forever. No groveling. No cooling off period. Instant forgiveness. Is there someone that Papa is calling you to forgive today? Have you had the Jesus filter applied to your heart?

#forgiven #clean#lookinggood #bestfilterever
#littleseedsofhope

Bear with each other and forgive one another if any of you has a grievance against someone. Forgive as the Lord forgave you.
Colossians 3:13

Forgiven by Crowder

DAY 31

There are times when my faith is weak and I've asked Papa God for a sign to get me through a tough spot and let me know He is real and cares. One time we were struggling financially and I prayed this in the morning. That afternoon we received in the mail a hundred dollar bill from a friend who said God told her to do it. Another time, we were in the middle of adopting Zayden and I was having a tough time with the social worker. I prayed, and the next day I received a letter from a co-worker whom I had not spoken to in two years. She said that she had no idea what I was going through but felt very strongly that God wanted her to write and encourage me. There have been times when I've prayed and have not had such an immediate and obvious answer. But usually just praying/admitting, "God, I'm weak and I need your help", makes me feel a little better. Then, I try to remember all the awesome things He has done for me because sometimes I'm ruled by emotion, can't think clearly and become short-sighted. I forget that I am Maria Belyea, daughter of The King of Kings, loved and cherished, the apple of His eye, gifted with strength, wisdom and peace, to do GREAT things! Beloved, if you are feeling discouraged today, please pray! Then, replace my name with yours. Say the words aloud and remember who you are and how much your Daddy loves you!

#helpmedaddy #openmyeyes #givemefaith #littleseedsofhope

For the eyes of the Lord are on the righteous and his ears are attentive to their prayer, 1 Peter 3:12

Give Me Faith by Elevation Worship

DAY 32

"Foye, have you ever thought about becoming a pastor?" We were standing in the living room of our house in Westerly, RI. Foye had just had a spiritual reawakening at a Promise Keeper's men's conference and was pursuing becoming a Connecticut state trooper. He looked at me and laughed, LOUDLY, "I'll become a pastor when Hell freezes over." "Ok," I said, but there was a whisper in my heart that disagreed. A year later Foye said, "I've been talking to Pastor Reggie and he thinks I should go to seminary." I'd like to say that I was supportive at first, but the opposite was true. I responded angrily, "So when Reggie tells you that you should become a pastor it's a good idea but when I say it it's funny?" Foye insisted that he still was NOT becoming a pastor, he just wanted to learn more. Yeah, right. In the winter of 1999, Foye became a licensed Minister of the Gospel. Many of his high school and college friends couldn't believe their ears and thought it was a joke because the Foye they knew was a rebellious rascal, a bad boy Marine and NOT a clergyman. Beloved, my faith grew exponentially as my husband slowly transformed from the inside out. What are your impossible dreams? Bring them to Papa God and have patience, sometimes answers are years in the making but miracles DO happen, and now a part of Hell is FROZEN!

#neversaynever #prodigalson #iwasright #justsayin
#stillarascal#littleseedsofhope
For no word from God will ever fail. Luke 1:37

God Of All My Days by Casting Crowns

DAY 33

When I read the verse below, my first instinct is to tell another story about the providence of God. But, what about the times when God doesn't do what we ask? Emilie was six years old when we went to an infertility specialist for the second time. Test after invasive test was inconclusive, so we decided to try more aggressive treatment and started hormone therapy. The injections made me angry one minute and weepy the next. They also made me feel like I was pregnant. Foye and I asked the church and all of our friends to pray that it would work. The Elders even laid hands on me and anointed my head with oil. After what felt like weeks of torture I went for a blood test. The results came when I was at nursing school and I remember it was raining. My cell phone rang as I was just about to leave one building to go to another. I ended the call, slid down the wall of the glass entryway until my butt hit the ground and sobbed. I was so very angry at God. Why had He abandoned and rejected me? I couldn't believe that after all of our prayers, He still said, "No." Friend, this is how I endured that painful time. I spent a lot of time reading the Psalms, particularly where David shares his pain and models how we can trust Papa God in the midst of trials. I shared my disappointment with our church family and asked for prayer. I counted my blessings. So many women NEVER get to experience childbirth even once and I had Emilie. Lastly, Foye and I began to think and pray about adoption. Beloved, I made a choice to have faith and believe that "God is good", although I don't always understand why or what He is doing. The simple truth is that even in dark times, I know that my life is better with Him in it and YES, I still believe He can move mountains.

#simplefaith #Godisgood #faithindarkness #blessed
#littleseedsofhope

Nothing is too hard for you. Jeremiah 32:17

Even If by Mercy Me

DAY 34

At our church, there's a part during communion where the Pastor says, "If you know you have wronged someone, then go to them and confess your sin. Make things right before you take communion." I think that confessing our sin in one of the hardest things to do. It's also one of the most cleansing. There are all different ways we can sin. The one I want to talk about is the sin of expectation. Have you ever had an expectation for someone that they didn't meet, and then you became hurt and angry? I have. There is someone in my life that had expectations for me that were disappointed. The irony is, I felt the same way about them. Every time the Pastor asks us to examine our hearts before communion I think of this person. I don't believe in coincidences. Jesus is laying their name on my heart. The problem is that after many years of hurtful words, we now barely speak and you know what? I like the silence, it's comfortable. In my heart I know that this is wrong. We may NEVER have a good relationship, but I need to own my part of the mess. Foye says that when you sweep things under the rug all you end up with is a landmine that someone will one day inadvertently step on. I have decided it is time to spring clean. I am going to spend time praying and asking God to make a way for me to have this difficult conversation. I am going to ask Him to make my hardened heart more compassionate and tender towards this person. Friend, is there a sin that you need to confess today? Maybe there is someone that you need to forgive. Every day is a chance for a new beginning. Will you join me in cleaning out the dark places where nasty spiders and even nastier sin likes to hide?

#forgive#confess #springcleaning #newday #littleseedsofhope

If we confess our sins, he is faithful and just and will forgive us our sins and purify us from all unrighteousness. 1 John 1:9

Jesus Friend of Sinners by Casting Crowns

DAY 35

Community involvement has always been super important to Foye. When we lived in Westfield, Massachusetts, he supported the local chapter of NAMI (National Association for the Mentally Ill) and was on the board of the homeless shelter. Both were vibrant and doing great work which brought larger than normal groups of homeless people to our town. As a result, we would be taking a walk on a beautiful spring evening, having a little date, and a homeless person would approach us wanting to chat with Pastor Foye. The first few times this happened, (and it happened a LOT) I was seriously annoyed. But then, I began to see a pattern. Foye knew most of the people by name. He always gave them a few minutes to talk before he explained that he was on a special date with his wife. During that time, they had his full attention. Foye actively LISTENED, repeated back to them what he heard and always responded with a few words to encourage and affirm them before excusing us. These encounters held a mirror to my heart. I realized I spoke too much and listened too little. These were people, not a problem. They were someone's son or daughter, and often felt lost and very, very lonely. Foye didn't try to impart any great pearls of wisdom. He didn't try fix their problems. Yet, beauty happened and a small measure of healing occurred with each conversation because he showed love.

#loveTOlisten #LISTENtoLOVE #lesstalkingmorelistening
#littleseedsofhope

Do not let any unwholesome talk come out of your mouths, but only what is helpful for building others up according to their needs, that it may benefit those who listen. Ephesians 4:29

If We Are The Body by Casting Crowns

DAY 36

I have this reoccurring dream that I am fixing up a house. Sometimes it's an enormous tree house. Other times it's a secret apartment that I find behind a hidden door. It ALWAYS needs a lot of work, but I can see the beauty under the peeling wallpaper and cracked paint. I am not working on the house alone. People from my life, past and present, are alongside me. I've come to realize that the house is an allegory for my life. I've always wanted my own home, one that I own and not a rental, somewhere that I can feel safe, find rest and BREATHE. The house also represents ME and all the people who have influenced my life. When you've been my shoulder to cry on it's like another wall has been given a fresh coat of paint. Hurtful words are like busted pipes that flood the kitchen and ruin my beautiful floors. I now know that there is no house that can satisfy this deep longing for peace and security, only Jesus can fulfill that role. He's also the Master Craftsman, renovating my heart, repairing my broken places into something new, something beautiful. There is no project too big or small for my Jesus. My prayer is that Jesus will make me into a showplace of His love and kindness, mercy and grace.

#builtbyjesus #NOjesusNOpeace #knowJESUSknowPEACE
#littleseedsofhope

There is no one holy like the Lord; there is no one besides you; there is no Rock like our God. 1 Samuel 2:2

Build My Life by Housefires

DAY 37

I was working at the clinic in Albany one very cold and windy Christmas Eve. My last patient was a tiny and frail elderly woman, and I asked her if she had any holiday plans. She said, "No, my friends are dead and my family doesn't live close by, so I'm going to go home and open a can of soup." My heart broke and I wanted to do something to help. Then, I remembered! We had a break-room FULL of food from the our holiday party. While the doctor did his portion of the office visit, I quickly packed up some leftovers. Then, I rushed into the social worker's office. Sometimes, people donated items for us to distribute. On Christmas Eve it was slim pickings. The only thing left was a box of crocheted afghans. We picked the prettiest one and even found a fancy bag to put everything in. Walking back to the exam room, I presented my little package with a cheerful Merry Christmas, full of pride from my good deed. The lady was so thankful that she burst into tears and said it was probably the only present she'd get that year. In that moment, my ego deflated as the enormity of her pain and loss FINALLY registered. Then, to my surprise, something unexpected happened. I was given a present too! It was the gift of humility.

#lovejustice #showmercy #walkhumblybeforeGod #littleseedsofhope

Let your conversation be always full of grace, seasoned with salt, so that you may know how to answer everyone. Colossians 4:6

Give Me Your Eyes by Brandon Heath

DAY 38

Early in our marriage, we were in a car driving somewhere and I said, "I think we should have some rules." Neither one of us was walking closely with Jesus at this point but we were committed to each other and wanted to make our marriage work. "Like what?" Foye replied, so I said, "Like not going to bars and getting drunk. People make stupid decisions when they are drunk and regret them later." "Ok." He said. I continued, "And not cursing at each other or saying things intentionally to hurt the other person. Even when you are angry, never say I Hate You or other words that you can't take back." The conversation went back and forth for a while as we shared things we felt would break our hearts and marriage. I don't remember everything we discussed but it felt like a sacred moment. We were taking a stand against evil. Friend, Satan is real and the Bible says he likes to KILL and DESTROY. Marriage is on the top of his hit list. Over the years, I've come to realize that preparing for danger is super important but what really saves a relationship is being a good runner. When temptation strikes, I make a beeline for Jesus because alone I am vulnerable and, at times, weak. Jesus is my strength and my protection. Beloved, do you have rules for your relationships? Have you prepared for danger? Is it time to get new running shoes?

#runtothecross #dangerzone #jesusstrong #littleseedsofhope

Submit yourselves, then, to God. Resist the devil, and he will flee from you. James 4:7

Broken Vessels/Amazing Grace by Hillsong

DAY 39

About halfway up the jet bridge after landing in Fort Lauderdale, my back went out. I stumbled and caught the wall or I would have fallen flat on my face. I tried to take a few steps carrying my computer bag and pulling my carryon, but pain stole my breath. Foye immediately walked over, slung my stuff on his back and slowly led me into the terminal. I realize that I rely on Foye's strength a lot but I know that if he hadn't been there God would have sent help. Three years ago, Foye had surgery right before we closed on our house in Voorheesville, NY. He couldn't lift anything and we had to pack, clean, paint and THEN move all of our stuff. I cried one night before bed, completely overwhelmed by the task. Foye, calm and full of faith said, "God will help us." I was skeptical. Painting day arrived and a few friends promised to help. I was hoping just to get the main living area done. To my surprise over a dozen people showed up. Neighbors, friends from church, and friends from the fire department painted our ENTIRE house. The same thing happened on moving day. It was miraculous and beautiful and grew my faith in Papa God and people. Beloved, do you have a burden or a task that seems overwhelming? Bring it to Papa AND don't be afraid to ask friends for help. He has brought us into each other's lives for a purpose.

#ineedyou #youneedme #createdforfamily
#littleseedsofhope

Praise be to the Lord, to God our Savior, who daily bears our burdens.
Psalm 68:19

Let Faith Arise by Bridge City

DAY 40

Our little dog, Luna, is a rescue. She was abandoned as a puppy under a bridge in Miami. Foye calls her a pest. She's headstrong, defiant, likes to hide and poop on my living room rug when it's raining because she doesn't want to get her feet wet (eye roll). She's also cuddly, silly, sweet and we ALL love her very, very much. We've been trying to train her to sit, stay and not to chew on people's hands. It's an uphill battle, because we are not always home and consistent. When I asked Jesus to be my savior, I was rescued and given a trainer called the Holy Spirit. However, JUST LIKE Luna, I don't always want to listen, I also hate getting my feet wet, may try to hide and have been known to carelessly chew on people. When Luna hides, I know exactly where she is and when she doesn't come I ALWAYS go to her. I am not going to abandon her and over time she will come to know this in her doggie heart. The Holy Spirit will never abandon ME either. He wants to help me grow and He is sooo patient even though I am willful and stubborn. Beloved can you relate? Are you hiding today? Life is too hard to attempt without training, without help. Come out of your hiding spot. If you do, I'm pretty sure there's a treat waiting for you.

#goodhuman #whereismytreat #nobiting #littleseedsofhope

For the grace of God has appeared that offers salvation to all people. It teaches us to say "No" to ungodliness and worldly passions, and to live self-controlled, upright and godly lives in this present age,
Titus 2:11-12

Spirit Of The Living God by Vertical Worship

DAY 41

Three years ago, a man was shot across the street from the clinic I managed in downtown Albany, NY. The nurses and I gave him CPR until the paramedics arrived. We kept the man alive, even though he was shot in the head, although he did eventually die at the hospital. Like an episode of Law and Order, a year later I was asked to testify. I was told not to be nervous, and just tell the truth about what happened. When I was finally called to the witness stand, it became quickly apparent that I was being accused by the defense attorney of running a "slow code." He implied that the man died because we really didn't try to save him. He didn't count on me being an excellent witness. In giving CPR, everything is timed. Therefore, I knew exactly how long it took before the police arrived (less than two minutes) and when the ambulance arrived (less than five minutes) because I remembered how many cycles of CPR we had completed. The truth is, it was actually miraculous that we had been able to keep the man alive at all. Just like that day in court, Jesus asks His followers to be witnesses for Him, to tell the story of what we have seen Him do in our lives. We don't have to be nervous, we don't need fancy words. If your life is a powerful testimony of the love and forgiveness of Jesus, share it! If we don't testify, then who will? How will anyone know The Truth?

#witness #tellyourstory #wordshavepower #mylifeischanged
#littleseedsofhope

But you will receive power when the Holy Spirit comes on you; and you will be my witnesses in Jerusalem, and in all Judea and Samaria, and to the ends of the earth. Acts 1:8

Testify by Need to Breathe

DAY 42

As a visiting nurse I get to go into some houses that are amazing... on the outside. The lawns are green and manicured, the exteriors are perfectly painted and maintained, and in the driveway are late model, expensive cars. Then I walk through the front door and see a DISASTER! Paint is peeling, trash and clutter are everywhere, the furniture is worn, dirty and falling apart. Sometimes there's even bug infestations. Beloved, the exterior of the house was really a beard, a disguise, hiding years and years of neglect. I was thinking about how people are not unlike one of these houses. We go to church in a nice outfit, smile, nod and pretend that everything is ok when inside it is NOT. Inside, our hearts are sick as we struggle with addictions or depression, anger or guilt. We clean up the outside because that's the part that everybody sees while our hearts are filled with trash. We let wounds fester. We don't seek help to repair the broken places and the craziest part is that after a while, we stop seeing the mess and it becomes our normal. Have you ever watched one of those fixer upper shows? Well guess what?! It's time for my favorite part, Demo Day! Let's get out the dumpster and haul out the trash. My heart could use some renovation and I have a Master Designer who loves to make broken places beautiful and NEW! Let's do it!

#Imabitofafixerupper #demoday #Jesusmakemenew #clean #littleseedsofhope

I will give you a new heart and put a new spirit in you; I will remove from you your heart of stone and give you a heart of flesh. Ezekiel 36:26

Set A Fire by United Pursuit

DAY 43

When I was 17 my mother tried to teach me to drive. It was an complete disaster. We'd both get angry, I'd end up crying and she'd be a nervous wreck. So, I asked my dad to teach me. He very wisely refused and I ended up having to pay for driving school. Back in those days there was no Siri or GPS and I got lost, a lot. I hated asking for directions and navigating with a map or a scrap of paper that said "turn left at the big tree" was excruciating. Being head strong is one of my greatest strengths and debilitating weaknesses. For a long time I struggled with submitting to authority, particularly if it was someone I knew. Asking for help tasted like failure. Of course this affected my walk with Jesus too. In the past, when I was going through a difficult time Foye would ask, "Have you spent time with the Lord? Have you prayed about it? Why don't you talk with that person who went through the same thing?" I knew he was right and rebelled against it. I wanted to figure things out myself, when I was ready. Beloved, I was never "ready" and my problems just got bigger along with my anxiety. It took until I was almost forty years old for me to be able to break the cycle, say the words, "I'm lost and need help" and finally let Jesus lead. It was SO freeing! Since that day, I've started to grow exponentially both personally and professionally. It may sound crazy, but I now feel stronger than EVER and I ask for help (and directions) ALL. THE. TIME. Friend, if you feel lost and exhausted today, pull over. Stop. Rest. Ask for directions. Maybe it's time to enjoy the view and let someone else drive.

#Jesustakethewheel #bestdecisionEVER #letgoandgrow
#Jesusstrong #littleseedsofhope

I will instruct you and teach you in the way you should go; I will counsel you with my loving eye on you. Psalm 32:8

Jesus Take The Wheel by Carrie Underwood

DAY 44

Emilie was 18 months old when I worked part time in the office of a nursing home. One day Foye brought Emilie to visit me at work. When I heard his distinctive voice in the hallway, I ran out of the office to greet them. What I saw shut down all my excitement and joy. To my horror, my husband had brought MY child, to MY PLACE OF WORK in an outfit that was mismatched! She even had two different color socks! I immediately started to dress Foye down (pardon the pun) in front of everyone. I wanted them to know that Maria Belyea, did not approve of this outfit! In the middle of my rant, one of the older nurses pulled me aside (thank you Jesus) and gave me a little set down. I'll never forget her words. *"Maria, no one cares if your daughter's clothes match. What we see is a loving daddy who brought his little girl to see her momma at work. If you humiliate him like that again, he will stop taking initiative and helping and that is something you will regret."* That day is burned into my mind and changed me. I cannot tell you that I have kept the lesson I learned perfectly, but I am a much better wife and mother than I would have been without it. When I read this verse today it made me think of those mismatched socks and how Foye is not controlled by anxiety and worry. Over the years I've watched him put his worries in a box, address that box to Jesus, put a stamp of prayer on it and send it on its way. One day I asked him in frustration, *"How can you do that?"* He said, *"Life doesn't stop because I'm worried and I won't let worry cripple me from doing what needs to be done. There's still a mission to be accomplished."* Beloved do you have a CARES package that needs to be sent to Jesus this morning? I do. It's a big one and here is my stamp of prayer: Help me Lord, you might have to actually pry this box from my hands. Jesus, I can't do this by myself. I want to learn, I want to grow, please can you send me your PEACE.

#carespackage #nofear #ichoosejoy #littleseedsofhope
"Therefore I tell you, do not worry about your life, what you will eat or drink; or about your body, what you will wear. Is not life more than food, and the body more than clothes? Matthew 6:25

Prince of Peace by Hillsong United

DAY 45

The night of my senior prom I missed curfew. This was WAY before cell phones, so my parents had no way of calling me or knowing where I was. I never called them to let them know I was going to be late because I assumed they would be in bed asleep. WRONG ASSUMPTION. We weren't doing anything bad, we just decided to go to the beach. Well...When I got home in the early hours of the morning, I opened the door to my house and there on the couch were my Father, Mother and two brothers all in a row with arms crossed, waiting for me. They had NEVER gone to bed! Immediately, I knew I was in big, BIG trouble. When I read the verse below, I thought about prom night. I substituted the words "your Dad" in place of The Lord and it put the verse in a whole new context. This isn't about fearing some big meanie in the sky who wants to zap you with a lightning bolt if you mess up. This is the fear I experienced when I disappointed my parents and damaged our relationship and trust by coming home over three hours late. I love them, didn't want them to be upset at me AND didn't want the consequences that they rightly imposed because of my disobedience. Papa God wants that same love and respect and gratitude for all that He has done for us. I remember my father being angry at one of us and saying, "I work hard all day to put food on the table and this is how you repay me?" It's no different with God. I imagine Him saying, "I've blessed you in so many ways. I even sent my son to die on the cross for your sins and this is how you repay me?" Suddenly, the sin that seemed so deliciously tempting a few minutes before, now tastes like cardboard. Friend, you are precious to God, beloved, the apple of His eye. Let's make our Papa proud today.

#youcandoit #chooseLOVE #itsaNEWday #makedaddyproud
#littleseedsofhope

The fear of the LORD is the beginning of knowledge, but fools despise wisdom and instruction. Proverbs 1:7

You Alone Can Rescue by Matt Redman

DAY 46

Labor Day 2008, a friend began a conversation with these words, "I know a little boy..." Ten months later, on July 18th, 2009, Papa God lifted up our heads and turned our tears into joy, laughter and a lot of really silly dancing because Zayden finally came home. That night, I sat in a rocking chair in my bra, holding Zayden against my skin so we would bond, humming into his hair, my lips pressed against those little brown curls so he could sense the vibrations (because he is profoundly deaf and doesn't wear his sound processors to bed) and felt like I had won the lottery. I was overflowing with gratitude and bursting with love for this child. This was my son! Here was living proof of God's goodness and faithfulness! Many of our friends were on their second and third babies and I thought I'd become invisible and God had forgotten me. I questioned whether it was something that we had done. Was Papa angry at us? Were we being punished? Beloved, Papa NEVER forgot ME and neither was He angry. I had forgotten that His plans are different from our plans and His ways are not our ways. Today, I am remembering the day we brought home our beautiful "Little Brown Biscuit" and I'm praising and thanking God for His faithfulness. My prayer is that Zayden's story would inspire you to HOPE! That his smile would fill you with joy and that your faith would be renewed in the goodness of our God, because He IS a good, good Father and we ARE loved by Him.

#chosen #childofmyheart #Godisfaithful #littleseedsofhope

Humble yourselves, therefore, under God's mighty hand, that he may lift you up in due time. 1 Peter 5:6

Good Good Father by Chris Tomlin

DAY 47

Emilie was just a baby and we needed to find a new place to live because our apartment had issues. Among other things, it was connected to the owner's garage. During the cold New England winter, they would let their car warm up inside and our apartment filled with exhaust fumes. We'd have to run and open all the windows so we wouldn't get sick. I prayed for God to help us, but the problem was that we could barely pay the bills. I was filled with crippling anxiety and fear about our future. One day, I was turning through the newspaper and saw a picture of a little yellow house and I heard God clearly say, "I'm going to give you a little yellow house." I ran to tell Foye who was skeptical. A few days later a family from church called us and said, "We have a rental property that's opening up and we'd like you to look at it." It was much more than we could afford but the owner told us not to worry, they would work something out. We drove up to the house and I burst into tears. It was the cutest little two bedroom yellow house. I keep this story in my pocket, and when I am anxious and worried I take it out to remember that Papa God loves me and nothing is impossible for Him.

#lovegrowsbestinlittlehouses #remember #faithbuilder #Papalovesyou #littleseedsofhope

Do not be anxious about anything, but in every situation, by prayer and petition, with thanksgiving, present your requests to God.
Philippians 4:6

Cast My Cares by Finding Favor

DAY 48

Recently, I had to forgive someone and for a moment I didn't want to. I was hurt and wanted to hang onto my anger. I wanted to tell everyone what they had done and how I had been wronged. I wanted them to hurt like I had been hurt. The pain felt like a softball in my stomach. But I knew that if I didn't forgive them, that softball would turn into a cancer that would eat me alive from the inside out with bitterness and anger. So I forgave them. Saying the words, "I forgive you", and actually forgiving someone are two different things. The words alone are often difficult to say but a lot of times we still hold a grudge in our hearts. As I've grown older, I've found that forgiving others has become a little easier. I know that's because I have made my own share of mistakes and caused harm. I know what it is like to go to someone, hat in hand, and say, "I'm so sorry." I also know what it is to be on the receiving end of unforgiveness. There is someone in my life that repeatedly brings up every perceived hurt and slight even after I've said I'm sorry. It's excruciating, like continually picking at a scab. My prayer is that when someone comes to me and asks for forgiveness I will be the person I want on the receiving end of one my apologies. In our family one of the things we say after we apologize is, "Can I have a new day?" Beloved, do you need a fresh start, a new day today? Go to Jesus. Pour out your heart. Confess your sin. His answer will always, ALWAYS be "Yes"!

#lifelessons #forgiven #newday #littleseedsofhope
Create in me a pure heart, O God,
and renew a steadfast spirit within me. Psalm 51:10

Freedom Hymn by Austin French

DAY 49

Cooking brings out my artistic side, a little bit of this, a little bit of that and voila! Dinner is served!! I love making recipes my own, trying out different flavor combinations. I never follow the recipe exactly. I might add a little more cumin or a lot more garlic and my cookbooks are marked up with my notes. I've discovered that baking is less forgiving. There's chemistry and science involved. If I am missing an essential ingredient my bread won't rise or my cookies will be hard as rocks. For me, losing weight has been a lot like baking. For years I tried to lose weight on my own but was unsuccessful. I didn't know it but I was missing essential ingredients. Then a friend shared with me her pain and struggles and invited me to a meeting about weight loss surgery. The doctor told story after story about people who had lost amazing amounts of weight and I realized that I was unsuccessful because I was missing some essential ingredients; accountability and HOPE. Did adding those ingredients into my life work? Over one hundred pounds later, I would say the proof is in the pudding. Do you feel hopeless and discouraged about an area in your life? Friend, perhaps you have forgotten the same ingredients I did. Beloved, it's a new day. Time to mix up a recipe for success! What changes have you been praying about? What ingredients do you need to win it today?

#notabaker #hockeypuckbrownies #spreadhope #itsjustlikebutter
#littleseedsofhope

Whoever pursues righteousness and love finds life,
prosperity and honor. Proverbs 21:21

I Am by Crowder

DAY 50

I had the middle seat on the plane the other day and I'm more of an aisle seat kind of girl. I like to make a fast getaway. On either side of me were big men, both asleep and lightly snoring. Honestly, I felt claustrophobic and a little fearful. I was waiting for one of them to put his head on my shoulder and drool. Hearing them snore made me think about what a leap of faith it is to fly. I got on the airplane without ever seeing the pilot or even knowing his name. At one point, I heard his voice over the intercom, but honestly that could have been a recording or done remotely. I saw his team, the flight attendants, but they were not the ones flying the plane. I even booked the ticket on a website without any human interaction. Then, I let this unknown, unseen person fly me ten thousand feet in the air. I found myself thinking about the irony of the situation. I can trust a total stranger with my life, but often have difficulty trusting Jesus with day to day problems. The two guys next to me were so comfortable and full of trust they fell asleep! If Foye had been flying with me, I might have fallen asleep too! Is it really that much harder to trust Jesus who I KNOW and have seen work time and time again? "Jesus, forgive me for doubting Your ability to care for my life. Here you go. I put my cares and worries in Your hands. Today, the only person I want to fly with is You."

#faithnotfear #hesgotthewholeworld #inhishands #littleseedsofhope

The life I now live in the body, I live by faith in the Son of God, who loved me and gave himself for me. Galatians 2:20

Trust In You by Lauren Daigle

DAY 51

Early in my career, I worked as a CNA while going to nursing school. Like many health care workers, I had to work every other Sunday, and I resented it because I had to miss church. I would drag myself out of bed and grumble the whole way to work. Then one Sunday, I had a patient who was dying of cancer. Her family had been with her all day and all night. Just as my shift started, they left to freshen up, all except for one son who gave me and my teammate permission to give his Momma a final bath. The woman was a Jesus follower and so was my fellow CNA, so we turned on the worship music the family had left in a tape recorder at her bedside and sang while we worked. That morning, I went to church in a hospital room with a dying woman. As we bathed her and spoke words of encouragement over her, the woman was semi-conscious but at the very end she awoke! She didn't speak but her eye grew wide as if she saw something amazing! Everyone in the room grew still and we felt the Lord's presence. I took the son's hand, put it in his momma's and said, "Tell her you love her. Tell her it's ok to go home to Jesus." We left the room as he did just that. I never resented working on Sundays after that. I had the privilege of preparing a Sister in Christ to meet the King of Kings. Through her eyes I had been given a glimpse of Heaven. I had forgotten that church is not just a building. It's not just four walls. It's all the people, from all over the world that love and trust Jesus.

#heavenisforreal #trustinjesus #divineappointments #littleseedsofhope

While he was blessing them,
he left them and was taken up into heaven. Luke 24:51

This Is Home by Switchfoot

DAY 52

If you know Foye you might find this story surprising. Eighteen years ago, we had just moved to Massachusetts for our first church. After just a few days, I noticed that he was feeling down. At first, he said nothing was wrong, but I knew my husband and finally my tenacity (nagging) wore him out. He admitted. "I really don't have friends. I have mentors and some acquaintances, but I would really like some guys that I can share with, quid pro quo." So I said, "Ok, let's pray about it, it's not a silly request. Maybe Jesus has laid that desire on your heart." In the middle of the backyard, I took Foye's hand and prayed a simple two sentence prayer. Looking back, I can see that God had already laid the ground work for the ABUNDANCE that was to come. A few days earlier, we had met a man named Jon who became one of Foye's dearest, most beloved friends. Since we that day, Jesus has blessed Foye with more friendships than he can count! If friends were dollars he would be a very, VERY rich man. It's a blessing that has even extended to our children, as our friends have loved on them too. What has Jesus laid on YOUR heart to pray about today? Maybe you are longing for friendship and community as well. Tell Papa, He IS listening.

#simpleprayer #BFFwithJesus #madetoLOVE #madetobeLOVED
#littleseedsofhope

May the Lord cause you to flourish, both you and your children.
Psalm 115:14

Love Has A Name by Jesus Culture

DAY 53

At times I struggle with letting Foye lead. I was tested this week when Zayden and the Young Marines spent four days learning boating and open water survival skills. Zayden has new cochlear sound processors and I was freaking out thinking that one or both of them would get swept away in the ocean. Replacement costs are over twenty thousand dollars. Several times a day I imagined every negative scenario, but guess what? Nothing bad happened. Zayden's processors and both my guys have survived, a little sunburnt, a lot exhausted, but happy and pleased with themselves. Me? I wasted four days worrying about something that I had no control over. I didn't trust Foye or God to take care of things. Maybe you are like me and agonize over things over which you have no control. I am asking Jesus for peace and the ability to surrender. I'm throwing up my hands and raising my white flag. Lord, I give up. I cannot control things. I need Your help to let go. I want Your peace to flood my system instead of stress hormones. Release me from the prison of worry and doubt. Help me to walk by faith and not by sight. Amen.

#jesustakethewheel #nofear #sorrybabe
#youwererightandiwaswrong #littleseedsofhope

I have told you these things, so that in me you may have peace. In this world you will have trouble. But take heart! I have overcome the world.
John16:33

White Flag by Passion feat. Chris Tomlin

DAY 54

Emilie and I love watching "Say Yes to the Dress." Poor Foye has even been subjected to an episode or two. I remember going with my mom to pick out my dress. I was so excited! Since that day, many years have passed, and marriage has been full of both love and disappointment. We are two imperfect people, held together because of the grace of Jesus. No fancy magical formula. Just Jesus. The Bible speaks of the church and Jesus, as THE Ultimate Bride and Bridegroom. However, Jesus is the ONLY Groom that will not fail you. He will not cheat. He will not abandon you (even when we act like Bridezilla). He will not throw you over for a younger better version of yourself. He knows you struggle with sin. He knows you don't always love Him back, if you ever loved Him at all...and yet He wants you and all your imperfections. He's crazy about you. He's preparing for you the home of your dreams. Will you say YES to Jesus today?

#sayyestothebest #threestrandchord #grace #bridezillachurch
#mansioninheaven #beloved #littleseedsofhope

Know therefore that the Lord your God is God; he is the faithful
God, keeping his covenant of love to a thousand generations of
those who love him and keep his commandments.
Deuteronomy 7:9

Beautiful Jesus by Jonathan and Melissa Helser

DAY 55

When we adopted Zayden the doctors did not know if he would ever walk normally, talk normally or even be able to read. Recently, Zayden took a Young Marines knowledge test. He wants to be promoted to Lance Corporal. It's the same fifty question basic knowledge test given to Young Marines who are in high school. He's eleven. He scored ninety-four percent. Young Marines is hard for my little dude. He has gross motor and language processing delays. Simply put, his muscles and his brain take a few extra seconds to warm up. He doesn't let that stop him. He has never, NEVER complained about the unfairness that he was born with what some might consider a disability or disadvantage. I don't think that it even crosses his mind. The other day he asked Foye, "Dad, am I a hard charger?" Foye answered, "Yes Bud, you're a hard charger." I wish you could've seen the beatific smile on my boy's face. When you feel like giving up, think of my little man. Let his story inspire you. Hear Papa's encouraging voice saying..."You can do it! I'm here with you! Don't give up! You're doing a great job! You're almost there! I am so, so proud of you!

#hardcharger#champion #papaisproudofyou #dearlyloved
#littleseedsofhope

Blessed is the one who perseveres under trial because, having stood the test, that person will receive the crown of life that the Lord has promised to those who love him. James 1:12

Courageous by Casting Crowns

DAY 56

For a long time Zayden was afraid of the dark. He doesn't wear his sound processors to sleep, so he wakes up in absolute silence and it's pitch black. That's scary, so we decided to buy him a nightlight and Foye found a small, framed picture of Jesus to put on the night-stand next to his bed. It's really a tiny little bulb, but it symbolizes hope and reminds him that morning is coming soon. When Zayden looks at his Jesus picture, he remembers that Jesus is with him and he doesn't have to be afraid because he is NEVER really alone. It worked great! Zayden woke up the morning after happy as a clam and said, "Mom I slept in my bed the whole night and was never scared!" As a Christian I feel like God is calling me to be like a night light in a really dark and scary world. However, my power source doesn't come from Florida Power & Light but from the TRUE LIGHT, Jesus. His light does more than dispel shadows. Jesus's light is a weapon against evil, it is a destroyer of death and can cast out fear. I know that my little bulb is a poor reflection of Jesus' magnificent ra-diance but I've learned from my son that even a tiny light can make a huge difference in someone's life.

#tinybutmighty #thislittlelightofmine ##shinejesusshine #littleseedsofhope

The true light that gives light to everyone was coming into the world.
John1:9

My Lighthouse by Rend Collective

DAY 57

A friend told me that he is an "eighty percent guy." He explained that he has difficulty closing deals. He has vision and can get eighty percent of the work done but then he chokes. I realized that this is my problem too. The end of a journey is usually the most difficult. I get tired, bored, the newness wears off and I've lost my passion. What was once exciting and energizing now seems like drudgery. In reality, I'm probably only a few steps from my goal. So, I asked my friend, who is a successful business person, what he does when he wants to quit. He said he has a team. People to come alongside, take off some of the load so he's not burned out and who will encourage and kick him in the butt when he needs it. He's right. Two of the people on my "Kick Maria's Butt into Gear Team" are Jesus and Foye. Maybe you are feeling all alone today and need a team of your own. Let me be your teammate today! "Do. Not. Give Up! You are soooo close! Just a few more steps!!" More importantly, cry out to Jesus. He has the real strength you need. It's as simple as, "Jesus, I need your help! I can't do this on my own!" He is the BEST team member that you could ever have.

#dontgiveup #80percenter #inHISstrengh #ipickJesus #littleseedsofhope

For everything that was written in the past was written to teach us, so that through the endurance taught in the Scriptures and the encouragement they provide we might have hope. Romans 15:4

Overcomer by Mandissa

DAY 58

Sometimes my patients make me feel like I am Super Nurse, battling against the monsters of Death and Disease with my trusty purple bag of magical potions and weapons. There's one particular elderly couple that are so excited to see me, they wait at the window and when I arrive they'll throw open the door and exclaim, "You're here!" Their relief is palpable as I walk in the room. As if we were in a comic strip, I imagine the bubbles of thoughts above their heads saying, "Help has arrived! Things will get better! Someone cares about me! Everything is going to be OK!" Beloved, have you ever felt like my elderly friends? Could you use a superhero to fight your monsters? Are you anxiously waiting by the window for help to arrive? Wait no longer! I've gotta' guy! He's THE Greatest Superhero of ALL Time. He's a mighty warrior! He can save the day AND He can save your life! He's already KICKED, Death and Destruction's booty TO. THE. CURB. Beloved, HE'S AT YOUR FRONT DOOR! Turn that knob and open it! Don't be afraid. He's a gentleman not a bully. Even though He's crazy strong and powerful, He's also gentle and kind and even tender to those he protects and serves. His name??? It's Jesus, aka Faithful and True, the Alpha and Omega, The Bright Morning Star, Lord of Heaven and Master of the Universe, and best of all ...Friend.

#JesusismyHero #deathisdefeated #Hesgotyou #NOMOREFEAR
#youareNOTalone #littleseedsofhope

My help comes from the Lord, the Maker of heaven and earth.
Psalm 121:2

Shout To The North by Robin Mark

DAY 59

It's three AM. I should be asleep, but it has been a rough week at our house. Foye has been working for Jesus in Haiti. Satan has also been working to make me miserable. Both have been successful in their endeavors. My mind is anything but peaceful as I lay here in bed. What I want to do is stress eat. The ice cream in the freezer calls me. Instead, I'm going to pray. People like to say "God doesn't give us more than we can bear." I don't agree. Sometime's, in this broken world, life just shovels it on and we CANNOT bear it. That's one of the reasons why we need Jesus! Beloved, if you are also feeling overwhelmed, please back away from the donut or whatever you use to self-medicate when life gets extreme. Join me in praying, "God, I need your help today. I'm exhausted and frustrated and cannot do this alone. Please pull me close to your calming Spirit and slow down my brain. Please resolve some of these things that keep me up at night." As I write, I hear a beautiful old hymn, redone by the band Jars of Clay. I am reminded that there is no shame in coming to Papa, in needing Him. It's just like when Emilie or Zayden come to me. I want to help them, to bless them. I look for ways to encourage them. Papa God is no different.

"I need Thee, oh, I need Thee; Every hour I need Thee;
Oh, bless me now, my Savior, I come to Thee.

I need Thee every hour, stay Thou nearby;
Temptations lose their pow'r when Thou art nigh."

#goodgoodfather #iNEEDtheeEVERYhour #missmyhubby #sleepplease
#littleseedsofhope

You will keep in perfect peace those whose minds are steadfast, because they trust in you. Isaiah 26:3

I Need Thee Every Hour by Jars of Clay

DAY 60

Recently, I was reading the story of David and Goliath. How incredible it must have been to see God move in such an amazing way. What a payoff for David's faith. However, I couldn't help but ask, "How could David fall so far from that moment that he kills a man in order to steal his wife?" I know why I fall away from God. It's because I forget. I forget what it felt like when I first asked Jesus to be my Savior. Back then I was full of gratitude, and my life goal was simply to please God. I forget all that He has done for me in the interim and fixate on the moment. I forget that Papa is the line leader (forgive my preschool analogy), and that I need to wait on Him to move. Our daughter, Emilie or "Belle" is now twenty-two years old. I see her full of passion and love for Jesus and I don't EVER want that to end. I don't want her to forget the last year when I saw God move powerfully in her life. This is the advice I gave her on her 22nd Birthday: Learn from the failures and successes of King David: 1. Follow THE line leader. Wait for Him to move before you take a step. 2. Remember. Remember. REMEMBER! Jesus is your first love. 3. You are a PRINCESS, a daughter of THE King. Don't forget who your Daddy is and He's made you BEAUTIFUL inside and out. Beloved. Those words are for you too.

#remember #princess #beloved #waitforit #littleseedsofhope

but those who hope in the Lord will renew their strength.
They will soar on wings like eagles; they will run and not grow weary,
they will walk and not be faint.
Isaiah 40:31

Lead Me To The Cross by Conrad and Conrad

DAY 61

Several years ago I went to Spain with a friend who is also named Maria. We become known as "Los dos Marias" or "The Two Marias." One day, we went to a town outside of Segovia for a feast day. On the green in the middle of the town was a tiny ancient church undergoing a restoration project. Master artisans were carefully peeling away paint and grime from the walls to reveal beautiful frescoes that had been hidden for centuries. I was transfixed. How incredible to think that I was getting to see something that had been hidden from human eyes for hundreds of years. Sometimes, I feel like that little church. Sorrow, suffering, and sin feel like 37 layers of paint. One of my favorite verses to pray when I'm feeling weighed down is Psalm 51:10. It says, "Create in me a clean heart oh God and renew a right spirit in me." Those words bring me so much peace. They imply that there's no sin that He can't wash away, nothing He can't forgive. He is THE Master Artisan, washing away the grime of life, making all those who seek Him beautiful. Jesus will you wash me and make me beautiful today?

#hemakesallthingsnew #beautiful #whiteassnow #littleseedsofhope
Therefore we do not lose heart. Though outwardly we are wasting away, yet inwardly we are being renewed day by day.
2 Corinthians 4:16

White As Snow by Jon Foreman

DAY 62

The other day our daughter Emilie scratched my car in the driveway. It was very tiny, almost imperceptible, but she felt terrible and worried that that I was going to be upset. I wasn't because twice (this is embarrassing) I have backed into Foye's car causing significant damage! In fact, right now he has a dinner plate sized dent in his left front quarter panel from my foolishness. Both times, Foye quickly forgave me. He was more concerned that I was ok than the state of his car. Our relationship was more important than the wrong. God loves you SO much more than Foye loves me. He wants to release you of everything that burdens your heart. I cannot tell you the relief I felt when Foye forgave me (especially the second time). A huge weight was lifted. Beloved, God does not want us to live under the shadow of guilt and shame. The Bible says He is slow to anger and abounding in love. His JOY is to take our failures and redeem them. I can't wait to take Foye's car to the body shop for repair. I know it will come out looking brand new, like my foolishness never happened. When God forgives us for our sins, it is also like it never happened. We may have earthly consequences, but it doesn't say ANYWHERE in the Bible that God is like Santa Clause, keeping a ledger of all the times you've been naughty and nice. Papa God has a parent's heart and just like I want to forgive Emilie, He wants to forgive us. All we have to do is ask.

#tradingmyshameforjoy #forgiven #giveittoJesus #littleseedsofhope

Have mercy on me, O God, according to your unfailing love, according to your great compassion blot out my transgressions. Wash away all my iniquity and cleanse me from my sin. Psalm 51:1-2

O Come To The Altar by Elevation Worship

DAY 63

A fledgling fell out of its nest. It hopped around our little front porch all day long, ignoring Momma bird, who squawked incessantly, trying to give it directions. Baby bird, curious about the world it had discovered below, was completely oblivious to the danger it was in. At nightfall, Momma bird went back to the nest to rest and care for her other children. All night long, the fledgling perched between the porch railings shivering and occasionally giving a pitiful cheep for help. I know this because I checked on it...often. In the morning, Momma bird flew back down and baby bird was more than ready to go home with her. Have you ever ignored Papa's voice and ended up in a dark place? I have and it wasn't very long ago. If that's you today, you don't have to wait until morning for help to arrive. Cry out to Papa. Listen for His voice. He NEVER sleeps and probably has already sent people into your life who love you and are just waiting to help. Remember, you are not in this alone. Ever. EVER. EVER!

#youarenotalone #youareloved #flyhomebabybird #littleseedsofhope

I am the Lord your God, who teaches you what is best for you, who directs you in the way you should go. Isaiah 48:17

Cry Out To Jesus by Third Day

DAY 64

I was at a Michael Card concert a few years ago and he told a story about a Chinese pastor who was imprisoned for preaching the gospel. They gave him the worst job in the prison to break his spirit, cleaning the sewage holding tank. The room smelled so awful they would leave him alone to do the job. He used the time to pray and sing praises out loud to the Lord. He called this filthy place his prayer garden and Michael Card joked that someone needed to write about it. I took that as a challenge. The Bible says that Papa delights in us and sings over us just like I have done with my children. I am SURE he was singing over this brave man. If you are feeling discouraged and down, listen. He is singing over you too.

> When darkness comes and all seems lost
>
> And hope feels like a dream you're clinging to
>
> Fear not, the Lord is here and He is singing over you.
>
> You are His child, His precious lamb
>
> He holds you safe within His hands
>
> His father's heart is filled with love for you
>
> Listen He is singing over you

#cesspoolprayergarden #praisehiminthestorm #lightupthedarkness
#littleseedsofhope

The LORD is close to the broken hearted
and saves those who are crushed in spirit. Psalm 34:18

There Is Power by Lincoln Brewster

DAY 65

When I was a young teen I was afraid of going to sleep. I thought that if I died in my sleep with unconfessed sin I wouldn't go to heaven. Each night I would wrack my brain trying to think of all the things I had done wrong and prayed that God would have mercy on my soul. Then I met Pastor Joel. He told me that when you give your life to Jesus and believe He is THE way, something crazy awesome happens. In that moment, Jesus obliterates ALL of the sins that you EVER committed and EVER WILL commit. Doesn't matter how bad they were, they are gone. Finito. Bye-bye. I believed him. I remember going to bed that night and having the startling realization that I could sleep without fear! It completely changed the way I prayed and the way I looked at God. Over time He went from scary judge, to my Papa. Jesus became best friend and big brother. Sunday night, Foye and I talked about crossroads in life. I KNOW I would be a completely different person without Jesus. Beloved, life is too short and difficult to be also burdened by fear, guilt and shame. Papa wants to give you His peace, His love and JOY! Life will still be hard. Bad things still happen. But knowing Jesus is at my side, walking through it with me, has made ALL the difference.

*#byebyesin #nottoolate #freedom #jesuslovesmethisiknow
#littleseedsofhope*

*Very truly I tell you, whoever hears my word and believes him who sent me has eternal life and will not be judged
but has crossed over from death to life.* John 5:24

Just Come In by Margaret Becker

DAY 66

I'm a nurse because the Holy Spirit used Foye to go down to Holyoke Community College, fill out an application and hand it to me to sign. I deeply regretted never finishing college before we married. I talked about going back all the time, but on my own I just couldn't take the first step. I was full of self-doubt and insecurities. Instead of focusing on all of the opportunities for success, I focused on the possibilities of failure. Do you have a dream today? Is there something that you feel God is calling you to do? I can't fill out an application for you, but I can encourage you! First, the voice in your head that's speaking words of discouragement and defeat is not from Papa God but the "other guy", so KICK HIM TO THE CURB!!! Second, write Philippians 4:13 (I can do all things through Jesus who strengthens me) on a piece of paper and stick it somewhere that you'll see it all day, like the back of your phone. Third, take one small step towards your goal today and then praise Papa for it and make plans to take another tomorrow. You can do this! You are worth it! You are beloved! He will make you strong! And remember the old saying, "How do you eat an elephant? One bite at a time." Bon Appetit!

#jesusstrong #saynotofear #dreambig #babysteps #littleseedsofhope

for it is God who works in you to will and to act in order to fulfill his good purpose. Philippians 2:13

Come As You Are by Crowder

DAY 67

My cutest/ugliest dog Luna loves to sleep. Foye has observed that in the evening she needs an extra nap to recover from her hard day of sleeping on the couch. I am NOT a good sleeper. I talk in my sleep, I have nightmares, and on rare occasions, night terrors. My human nature is to worry and fix. I give Jesus my problems, but then I try to take them back. It can get tiring playing spiritual tug of war. So how do I find any rest? I was thinking in the shower this morning (I do some of my best thinking there), that I live like life is a puzzle to be solved when it's more like an obstacle course, a US Marines, nasty, dirty obstacle course. I'm restless (anxious) because I'm trying to do it alone when I need my big brother Jesus, THE ROCK, to run next to me, give me a boost to climb those walls, and help carry my pack when I'm tired. Maybe He even needs to carry ME! No wonder I'm exhausted! So here it goes..."Jesus, sorry for being so stubborn. I'm ready to buddy up. I've got nothing left. Ummm..could you carry me TODAY because Luna and I really need to take a nap."

#iknowTHERock #napsAREawesome #jesusstrong #littleseedsofhope

*Come to me, all you who are weary and burdened,
and I will give you rest.*Matthew 11:28

Carry Me by Josh Wilson

DAY 68

At twenty-one years old, three quarters of the way through college, I dropped out. I had no idea what I wanted to do when I grew up and I was in love. I always planned on going back, someday. However, someday never came. First it was planning for a wedding, then a baby, then bills and work and... life. When we moved to Albany, NY, I would pass the University at Albany almost every day. I began to pray for God to make a way for me to go back to school. I didn't know where the money was going to come from, and I had no idea how I was going to juggle my full time jobs as a nurse, pastor's wife and Mommy, but I went online and filled out the application. Beloved, I got in and God provided the money, but college was HARD. I wanted to quit so many times. I almost dropped out the last semester because I was exhausted. Jesus had other plans. When I wanted to give up, He surrounded me with people who loved me enough to give me a kick in the pants and get me back on track. Friend, are you exhausted today? Does the finish line seem miles away and you're running out of gas? Guess what? You are absolutely right, so STOP. Take a moment and pray a simple SOS prayer like, "Jesus I need Your help." Let the Holy Spirit fill your tank. This is your loving kick in the pants! "You are not allowed to quit. It's time to pray! Ask Jesus for helpers and then – this is the most important part – accept their help! Remember, all you have to get through is today."

#cheerleader #lookforthehelpers #almostthere #onedayatatime #WEgotthis #littleseedsof hope

Now to him who is able to do immeasurably more than all we ask or imagine, according to his power that is at work within us,
Ephesians 3:20

Holy Spirit by Francesca Batistelli

DAY 69

In my final semester of nursing school I decided I wanted to be an Operating Room Nurse at Baystate Medical Center, a level one trauma hospital. There was just one problem, Baystate NEVER hired new grads into their OR, or so the director kindly explained to me. I was undeterred and pestered that woman until finally she relented and gave me a job. (Happy dance!) A few days later Foye came home from church and said, "My father is sick. I've been praying and God is calling us to move to Florida." I was so angry with both my husband and God. Didn't they know how hard I had worked? We were finally going to buy a house! I was going to hire a cleaning lady!!! Arhhhhg! It took me a while to put aside my anger and see that God's plan was better than anything I could have imagined. Foye's dad really did need us and the friendships I have made as a result of that move I would not trade for any job or cleaning lady in all the world. I take this story out of my pocket when I don't understand what Papa God is doing and remember that He alone sees the big picture and I can put my trust in Him.

#iwilltrustinyou #whereveryougo #iwillfollow#stillnocleaninglady #littleseedsofhope

*In their hearts humans plan their course,
but the LORD establishes their steps.* Proverbs 16:9

Oceans by Hillsong United

DAY 70

I was at a friend's house for a party when I swallowed a piece of steak that was too large. Instead of asking for help I foolishly took a drink which only further lodged the meat in my throat. An eerie calm came over me and I began to have an internal conversation, completely detached from the urgency of the situation. FINALLY, when I felt myself start to lose consciousness, I decided to let Foye know I needed help and touched his leg. He was sitting RIGHT NEXT TO ME. He took one look, jumped up and quickly performed the Heimlich maneuver. He saved my life. I asked him later how he knew I was in trouble. He said, "You were drooling and I knew you would NEVER drool in public." I thought about this situation a lot. How could I have felt so calm and in control when the exact opposite was true? Why did I wait until the last minute to ask for Foye for help? I realized that I have difficulty trusting people and I almost died because I convinced myself I had everything under control. Friend, do you feel like you are spiritually choking? Are you trying to do this life all on your own? Reach out to Jesus. He wants to help you when you've bitten off more than you can chew. Trust Him with what's on your heart. Ask Him for friends to help carry the load. We were not meant to go through this life alone, and control is an illusion. We need each other. We need Jesus.

#notincontrol #ineedyou #youneedme #weneedjesus #littleseedsofhope

For God so loved the world that he gave his one and only Son, that whoever believes in him shall not perish but have eternal life.
John 3:16

How Can It Be by Lauren Daigle

DAY 71

When my brother Joseph was little we lost him in a large grocery store. My frantic mother alerted the store manager and everyone began to search. I stood at her side terrified. After over an hour he was found, not more than twenty feet from the checkout counter, in a booth that played cartoons (similar in construction to a photo booth). My poor mother was LIVID!!! She and the entire store had been calling his name and he ignored them. Sometimes I am exactly like my little brother, only the person I ignore is the Holy Spirit. He tells me to do things that I don't want to, like showing kindness and love to someone who irritates me or forgiving someone who has hurt me or volunteering at church when what I really want to do is sleep in and watch Netflix. He's tricky that Holy Spirit. He uses songs on the radio, Bible verses I've memorized and sometimes MY OWN CHILDREN to convict my heart! But, every time I obey, I am incredibly blessed and so happy I did! Are you hiding under the covers where it's safe? Papa has blessings for you today. Will you join me in saying, "Here I am Jesus, use me."

#lostandfound #chooseblessing #sayyestothebest #butmybedissocozy
#littleseedsofhope

Your word is a lamp for my feet, a light on my path. Psalm 119:105

God With Us by Jesus Culture

DAY 72

Like a lot of kids I was bullied in school, so I escaped into books and dreamt about one day becoming a foreign correspondent who went undercover to expose wrongs and bad guys. I wanted to be tough and fearless. Totally. In. Control. Then one day a woman came to our church and in my eyes she was everything I was not. Soft spoken and gentle, I felt better just being around her. She exuded the peace of Christ like one of those fancy essential oil diffusers. My blood pressure went down just standing next her. As I got to know her better I realized that she was not a pushover or weak in ANY way. She just relied on Jesus for strength. She knew that whatever happened, Jesus had her back and would get her through, especially when the outcome was not what she hoped for. When I read the verse below I immediately thought of her. Her soft words were more effective than any angry outburst. Her kindness more effective to break down walls than any Bible verse delivered with a karate chop. Back then I asked God if I could grow up to be just like her. He said, "No. Be you. I love you. I made you. But...be the best sassy version of you, the one that puts her faith and trust in me." That is definitely something I can work on.

#sassyforjesus #kindnesswins #showlove#littleseedsofhope

A gentle answer turns away wrath, but a harsh word stirs up anger.
Proverbs 15:1

Mountain by Brian and Katie Torwalt

DAY 73

Without my glasses I cannot see the nose in front of my face. No seriously, I can't see my nose, it's just a flesh colored blur. It's part of the gift of being in my forties. I literally put on my makeup every morning blind and then have to clean up the mess I make with Q-tips. The irony is that in my forties my spiritual vision has become so much clearer. There's wisdom that comes from years of trial and error. One of the most important things I have learned is that if I don't spend time with Papa God in prayer and really know what He says in the Bible, it's like I'm driving at night without my glasses, which would be very scary. The beautiful thing is that even a few minutes in the morning begins to clear my vision. I find that much of life is difficult. Obstacles are everywhere, I am naturally klutzy and have a poor sense of direction. However, when I put on my spiritual glasses of prayer, worship and reading God's word...all the confusion falls away and my priorities, my goals, my purpose become crystal clear. There are many things that I REALLY dislike about getting old, like gray hair, wrinkles, arthritis! Ugh! However, clearer spiritual vision is something that I am very, VERY thankful for. Try it! Start with just a few minutes a day. You might like what you see!

#fortiesarefabulous #amazinggrace
#IwasblindandnowIsee#littleseedsofhope

"Hear, you deaf; look, you blind, and see! Isaiah 42:18

Amazing Grace My Chains Are Gone by Chris Tomlin

DAY 74

I was working in the hospital on the night shift and a few of us were sitting at the nurses station. One of the nurses started talking about being a Christian and going to church. I hadn't really been listening to the conversation up to this point, but I felt obligated to say, 'I'm a Christian too, my husband is a pastor." The woman looked at me in shock. "You're a Christian? I had no idea. You never said anything." It felt like a kick in the gut. I had been working with these nurses for almost a year! I went home in deep contemplation. How did I let this happen? I realized that because I didn't love my job and staying up all night was really hard for me, I had been keeping my head down, grinding through the shift and not really interacting with others. As a result, I had missed a lot of opportunities to share my faith, to share the hope of Jesus. I also acknowledged that no one would have listened to me because I was completely focused on the negative and living like I was being punished not blessed. That day, I made a commitment to change my attitude and not let circumstances determine my joy. I began to see challenging situations as opportunities to make Jesus shine. I worked on building friendships and listening instead of tuning my colleagues out. I vowed to never forget that the hospital wasn't my boss, Jesus is.

#letyourlightshine #thedevilcantstealmyjoy #JesusisTHEboss
#secondchances #littleseedsofhope

And whatever you do, whether in word or deed, do it all in the name of the Lord Jesus, giving thanks to God the Father through him.
Colossians 3:17

Joy by For King and Country

DAY 75

Some of the best marriage advice I ever received was from my Grandma "Gigi" right before I got married. She said, (this is a paraphrase because I don't remember the exact words and half of it was in Spanish), "If you and Foye have an argument don't tell everyone. Find a close friend to ask advice and share your heart with. Protect his reputation. You will forgive him because you love him and know his heart. Other people will just tally up the wrongs." This was perfect advice for me because I am an external processor (I think best by talking a problem out) and I am sensitive and can get angry quickly, particularly when I was younger. It could have been really hard to follow if God had not sent me godly women to guide me. Many times I was upset about things that weren't wrongs at all, just misunderstandings and miscommunications. Many times these women talked me off the ledge and gently helped me to see my part in the situation. I have no doubt that part of the success of our marriage is directly attributable to these wonderful friends. If they had been negative, kept a list of all the slights that I had perceived Foye to do and reminded me of them over and over, our marriage would have not survived. Friends if you did not have a "Gigi" to give you this loving advice, it's not too late AND it's not just for marriage but all of our relationships. Throw away that list of mistakes. Forgive. Show love. See your part in the mess. If Jesus doesn't hold grudges then how can we?

#Ilovemygrandma #gigiknows #seventytimesseven #Jesusforgaveme
#thankyou #littleseedsofhope

My dear brothers and sisters, take note of this: Everyone should be quick to listen, slow to speak and slow to become angry, James 1:19

New Wine by Hillsong

DAY 76

Foye told me a beautiful story that I have been wanting to share. He was at WAWA waiting to have a lunch meeting when he noticed several homeless people. One particular gentlemen appeared to be mentally ill and was talking to himself. Foye watched as a younger man, also homeless, bought a sandwich and sat at a table to eat. The man that was talking to himself sat down next to this young man and Foye's heart was touched when he watched him break his sandwich in half and tenderly share it. That night we marveled at how it is often the people who have little that are the first ones to share. I reflected on how at times I have been stingy with sharing my faith. I've worried about what other people will think. I've worried that I won't have the right words and will sound stupid. I've worried that someone might call me a hypocrite because they know how I struggle with sin. I forget that I have done nothing to earn Jesus' peace, joy and love, which are infinite gifts that will never run out no matter how much I give away. Thank you Jesus for all that you have given me. Friend, would you like half?

#sharejesus #foodforthesoul #leastofthese #littleseedsofhope

When anxiety was great within me, your consolation brought me joy
Psalm 94:19

Leave Your Sins At the Door by Maria Belyea

DAY 77

A friend bought a new washer and dryer and wanted the old ones to go to someone in need. He put them at the curb with a sign that said twenty dollars. The next morning the washer and dryer were both gone. I asked him if he was upset that someone had stolen from him. He said, "No. I would have given them away, but I've put things out with a FREE sign before and no one took them because they assumed it was worthless junk." I get this. I love a bargain, but I won't spend a penny until I am convinced that what I'm purchasing has value. I think that sometimes people discount the value of being a Christian because we say that grace is free when it's really more like a very, very, VERY uneven trade. You give King Jesus, Who is the creator of the universe and infinite Almighty God, all of your dirty sin, all of your shame, all of your pain and sorrow. In return He gives you the treasures of peace, hope, joy, rest, salvation and the promise of eternal life that He purchased at the cross (plus a bunch of other awesome, mind blowing, and priceless stuff). I've heard people call this impossible and incredible exchange, reckless love. They are right! Except, nothing is impossible for God and like any loving parent, He will move mountains to get to the one He loves. YOU!

#BESTbargainEVER #treasuresfortrash #makethetrade #recklesslove
#littleseedsofhope

I am the Alpha and the Omega," says the Lord God, "who is, and who was, and who is to come, the Almighty." Revelation 1:8

Diamonds by Hawk Nelson

DAY 78

At our house on Long Island my dad had a lovely garden. One of his favorite things to grow were yucca plants. Unfortunately, my mother hated them because they attracted bugs and she thought they were ugly. One morning after he left for work, mom took out the gardening tools. I remember her hacking and digging for hours until all of the yuccas were gone! That evening, Dad came home from work and went to water his plants. I held my breath. After a little while he came back, nonchalantly washed his hands and sat down for dinner. We ate in total silence, staring at him until finally my mother couldn't take it anymore and said, "Joe, did you see what I did to the yucca plants?" Without missing a beat, he looked at my mother and asked (with a little chuckle in his voice), "So how far down did you dig?" Apparently, yuccas are SUPER hardy. They can grow roots 20 feet deep because they want the richest, most nourishing soil AND each little piece of root left in the ground can sprout into a new plant. This was evidenced a few weeks later when our house was surrounded by dozens and DOZENS of little baby yucca plants. When the Bible talks about being rooted in Christ, in my head I hear, "Go deep like a yucca plant and when the storms of life come and things on the surface seem bleak, your faith won't be shaken. In fact, those deep roots will sprout and grow more faith (like little baby yucca plants), as you allow Jesus to nourish and sustain your heart and soul."

#yuccaplantsforever #daddywon #sorrymom #multiplyfaith
#littleseedsofhope

I am the resurrection and the life. The one who believes in me will live, even though they die; John 11:25

Mention Of Your Name by Jenn Johnson

DAY 79

When I was a little girl my father fell down a flight of stairs while carrying me on top of his shoulders. As a result, I am terrified of heights. I hate rollercoasters. When we go to the amusement parks I am the stuff holder. My husband is the complete opposite. He LOVES rollercoasters! The bigger the fall, the bigger the thrill. On a trip to the coast, when Emilie was little, we stopped along a rock wall bordering a steep drop down to the ocean. Emilie said, "Daddy, pick me up! I want to see!" Foye, to my horror, put her up on the wall and held her hand as she happily walked along, enjoying the beautiful view. I felt sick to my stomach and couldn't even watch. I begged him to take her down. He refused, saying, "I've got her hand. I won't let anything happen to her. She is safe." When I read the verse below I remembered Emilie walking that wall with arms outstretched, happy as a clam and I thought, "I want that. I want to live life unafraid. I want to enjoy the view. I want to trust that Papa has my hand and I am safe." Do you have a rock wall that you need to walk with Papa? I do and I'm ready to take a few steps. Will you join me? Deep breath! Take Papa's hand and GO!

*#holdingdaddyshand #safe #nofear #trustintheLord #faithlikeachild
#littleseedsofhope*

*Trust in the Lord with all your heart and lean not
on your own understanding; Proverbs 3:5*

Fearless by Jasmine Murray

DAY 80

I was nineteen the Christmas after my parents separated and money was so tight that we couldn't even afford a Christmas tree. This really upset my mom, so she prayed and asked God for a tree. Honestly, I didn't think God cared about stuff like that. The next morning one of our neighbors came by while my mom was at work and said, "I noticed you don't have a Christmas tree and I'd like to buy you one and any decorations you need." I started to cry. I thought that surely this was the answer to my mother's prayer. We went down to the tree lot, picked a lovely tree and had it all set up to surprise my mom when she got home. That evening my mom came home all excited and she hadn't even seen the tree yet. "Guess what!" she said. "There was a raffle at work and I won a free Christmas tree!" Then we heard a knock at our back door. No one was there but on our porch was ANOTHER Christmas tree! God had sent us THREE Christmas trees! That day I was taught an important lesson. Papa God listens and cares about EVERYTHING. What is on your heart today? Bring it to Papa. Nothing is impossible for Him.

#prayBIG #smallstuffmatters #mustardseedfaith #littleseedsofhope

And do not forget to do good and to share with others, for with such sacrifices God is pleased. Hebrews 13:16

You Are For Me by Kari Jobe

DAY 81

I used to attend a Pastor's wives retreat on the shore of Lake Winnipesaukee. On the third day we would pack a lunch and get dropped off by boat on Rattlesnake Island for three hours of silent contemplation and prayer. It was very difficult for me. I'd sit down in the woods with my Bible and journal and try to hear God's voice, but my mind was so full of noise it would take at least an hour before I could settle and then I often fell asleep. I stunk at silence. I am reminded of the time when Jesus took His closest disciples away for a time of prayer and silence. They fell asleep too! That's because they struggled with all the same things we do. They were ordinary, average men and yet God used them to do extraordinary and amazing things. It gives me hope! If God could use a bunch of cranky fisherman to change the world, surely He could use this opinionated, Long Island Princess who needs to talk less and listen more.

#lesstalkingmorepraying #Lifegoals #practicelistening #canitalkyet #littleseedsofhope

Even fools are thought wise if they keep silent and discerning if they hold their tongues. Proverbs 17:28

Dry Bones by Lauren Daigle

DAY 82

A ride in a NY City taxi cab can be a frightening experience. I was riding with a friend who had never been to The City before. As we whizzed through traffic my terrified friend jumped onto my lap! She said that if we died she wanted to make sure she was going to heaven and hoped that since I was a pastor's wife I had a direct line to God. Sometimes people think that Pastors have a "Bat-phone." You know, the special phone that commissioner Gordon used to contact BATMAN! Well, I'll let you in on a little secret...we do! It's called Prayer! AND if you've given your life to Christ, the Bible says that you too have a "Bat-phone" directly to Father God! This is the way it works. It's not high tech. You just say, "Hi Dad" and then you tell Him what's on your heart. You don't have to be a pastor or a pastor's wife or even a pastor's kid to pray. God doesn't look at our education, our bank account, or whether we have a criminal record. He doesn't care if we're male or female, an adult or a child. The ground is level at the foot of the cross. Friend, I LOVE it when Emilie calls from college to ask a question, for advice or just to say that she loves me. Papa God is no different. He LONGS to hear your voice! Beloved, what are you waiting for? Send up that "bat signal" and call your Daddy in heaven today.

#iambatgirl #ihaveabatphone #unlimitedprayingplan #perks
#littleseedsofhope

If you declare with your mouth, "Jesus is Lord," and believe in your heart that God raised him from the dead, you will be saved.
Romans 10:9

Give Me Jesus by Jeremy Camp

DAY 83

One Sunday, many years ago, when I was going to nursing school I had a patient who was dying of AIDS. He was dirty because some of the other staff were afraid to catch his disease. I felt such compassion. I wanted this man to die with dignity, so I got some towels and hot, soapy water and went to work. Something mystical happened when I washed that man. I felt like I had been transported to Jesus' time and was not washing some stranger's body but the actual body of the crucified Christ. Thank goodness the man was unconscious because I imagine it would have been upsetting to see your nursing assistant crying over your hands and feet, but all I could think about were the women lovingly preparing Jesus's body for burial, their tears mixing with the herbs and spices. It's a day I will never forget. I was so humbled. Here I thought I was doing this man a favor, instead he ministered to me. I do not know what happened to that poor man, but am hoping that he put his faith and trust in the Resurrected Savior and is now walking and laughing in heaven, free from disease and pain.

#chainbreaker #jesuspaiditall #alltohimiowe #feetwasher #HeisRisen #iamfree #jesusisreal #trustjesus #littleseedsofhope

He is not here; he has risen, just as he said. Come and see the place where he lay. Matthew 28:6

Chain Breaker by Zach Williams

DAY 84

Upon learning that I have an adopted child a woman asked me who he looks like. I replied, "He looks just like his Dad." Zayden may have brown skin, while Foye is pink (according to Zayden), but in all the ways that matter, Zayden looks EXACTLY like his daddy. He loves all the things that his dad loves. He's picked up his mannerisms and phrases. If you spent five minutes talking with Zayden, you would easily be able to determine that he is Foye's son. This is because Z wants to spend every waking moment at Foye's side. Even at night his preferred place to sleep is in a nest of blankets next to our bed. When Foye is away it's, "Daddy said this, and Daddy said that, and I wonder what Daddy is doing?" NONSTOP. I am learning from Zayden's example and spending more time with Papa God than I ever have in my life and guess what?! I am growing to love both Him AND the people He loves more and more each day! I look forward to talking with Him and reading His word. I want to sing to Him, I want to share my heart with Him in prayer. My goal is that when people see me they will say that I look just like my Dad too.

#twins #likefatherlikeson #daddysshadow #lifegoals #littleseedsofhope

And if the Spirit of him who raised Jesus from the dead is living in you, he who raised Christ from the dead will also give life to your mortal bodies because of his Spirit who lives in you. Romans 8:11

To Live Is Christ by Sidewalk Prophets

DAY 85

Zayden has a ticklish spot on his neck. He calls it "my weakness", like he's a superhero and that's the chink in his armor. In reality, as an adopted child, my sweet boy's real weakness is that he struggles with fear of abandonment. When Foye goes away on a business trip this is most evident. I have to reassure him over and over that Daddy loves him and is coming back. He wants to know the exact date and time and literally counts the minutes until his return. I am not adopted, but I too have a "weakness." When things don't go the way I expect or plan, I have to work at not listening to the Father of Lies who says, "God doesn't love you. You're being punished. You need to figure out a way to fix this. The only person you can count on is yourself...." To combat the forces of evil I turn on worship music, and listen instead for the voice of truth, the Holy Spirit, who says, "I love you. You are precious to me. I have a hope and future planned for you. I will help you through this. You are not alone. The weight of the world is not all on you."

#myweakness #fearISaLIAR #beloved#mysonisasuperhero #phew
#littleseedsofhope

When I am afraid, I put my trust in you. Psalm 56:3

Do It Again – Elevation Worship

DAY 86

One night before bed, when Emilie was a very little girl, not even three years old, she said, "Momma, how do I know God is real if I've never seen him or touched him?" This is a not a conversation that I ever imagined having with a toddler, but then again she is Foye's daughter. I'm surprised she didn't say, "Mother how can I be assured that belief in an omniscient being is not a false construct of my infantile psyche to validate my need for significance?" I'll admit to being was momentarily blindsided and a little freaked out. I sent up an SOS prayer and the answer immediately came. "Can you see air? Yet, we believe air is real because we breathe it and when we blow it into a balloon we can watch the balloon grow. It's the same with God. We can know He's real because we can see the things He does." I have come to realize that this little lesson was more for ME than Emilie. I have revisited it many times when I am dealing with anxiety, fear and doubt. Do you ever wonder if God is real? Is He just a figment of our imaginations? When I doubt, I picture a shiny red balloon. It represents all the ways that I have seen God work in both my life and the lives of others and just like the sun piercing through the clouds, faith pierces through my doubt and I BELIEVE.

#faithnotfear #balloonsarecool #apologeticsfortoddlers
#takesafterherdaddy #littleseedsofhope

Whoever has my commands and keeps them is the one who loves me. The one who loves me will be loved by my Father, and I too will love them and show myself to them." John 14:21

Need You Now by Plumb

DAY 87

Zayden did not walk until he was two and a half years old which is when we adopted him. He was a big boy too, around forty lbs. of beef. Foye and I made the decision after reading a book on toddler adoption that we wouldn't let anyone else carry him or feed him for the first three to six months so that he would bond with us. We didn't take into account how much he weighed and how tiring it was to lug that little brown biscuit around. Zayden may not have been able to talk but he communicated just fine. When he was tired of walking, which was often, he would either fall down on the ground and not move OR put his arms up to be carried. He LOVED being carried and was so darned cute that I carried him A LOT! As a result, we were able to bond with our son and he with us and on a side note, I had THE BEST arm muscles that year. Beloved, are you tired? Do you need to be carried like Zayden in the arms of Papa today? The Bible says just reach out your arms and He will gather you to His chest like a momma hen gathers her chicks, tucking them safely under her wing. Don't feel guilty for growing tired and weary. It was always part of His plan for us to find rest in Him.

#daddylovesme #mommamuscles #boymomma #underhiswing #safe #littleseedsofhope

Do you not know? Have you not heard? The Lord is the everlasting God, the Creator of the ends of the earth. He will not grow tired or weary, and his understanding no one can fathom. Isaiah 40:28

It Is Well by Bethel Music

DAY 88

For those of you who don't know Foye well, my tough Marine is a big 'ol softie when it comes to his babies. Case in point, the other day I came home to find Zayden watching a movie when I knew he was punished and not supposed to be watching anything with a screen. (The threat of "No screens" is one of my most effective ways to encourage my son to make a better choice.). "Why is Zayden watching TV?", I asked Foye in probably not a nice voice. He answered, "Because I want him to understand what God's grace looks like in real life." At first I was annoyed because of course I was the one who had taken away the privilege, but then MY heart softened because I remembered that Jesus has cancelled the debt of every sin I have ever committed. How could I begrudge my son a taste of what is freely given to me, EVERY DAY. So instead of making a fuss, I popped some popcorn, made like Elsa and let it GO!

#iamfree #nocondemnation #passthepopcorn #daddyisabigsoftie
#littleseedsofhope

Therefore, there is now no condemnation for those who are in Christ Jesus, because through Christ Jesus the law of the Spirit who gives life has set you free from the law of sin and death. Romans 8:1-2

Grace That Is Greater by Building 429

DAY 89

A few years ago I had a spot on my breast that wouldn't go away. My doctor, concerned that it was cancer, had me make an appointment with a surgeon. Foye was worried and wanted to ask the church for prayer, but I said. "No." I didn't want to make it public. I didn't want to talk about it because I was afraid and if we didn't talk about it, then it wasn't real. When the surgeon scheduled a biopsy, Foye asked again if he could go to the church for prayer. I relented, not because I was full of faith, but because I knew it would make him feel better. That Sunday the congregation prayed for me. It was uncomfortable and overwhelming. It also felt nice to know that all these people cared about me. A couple of days later I had to call the surgeon to ask if she still wanted to do the biopsy because the spot on my breast was completely gone. If you have an area of your life that needs prayer, don't hesitate, RUN to someone for prayer! Prayer is THE MOST POWERFUL TOOL WE HAVE against all that is wrong in this world. I almost missed an incredible blessing. Thank you Papa for my husband's faith and obedience. It saved my life.

#lessonlearned #prayerchangeseverything #healed #mustardseedfaith #littleseedsofhope

Therefore confess your sins to each other and pray for each other so that you may be healed. The prayer of a righteous person is powerful and effective. James 5:16

Hold Me Jesus by Rich Mullins

DAY 90

On our very first date, Foye plucked a red tulip from our college dean's garden, kissed my hand like a gallant knight and presented it to me. After admonishing him for stealing the flower, I was smitten. I still have the dried tulip petals preserved in my box of special things. A few weeks later he told me that he loved me. Neither of us had any idea about the weight of those words. Recently, I've become curious about the word love and why/when people began to say "I love you" to one another. Love seems like such an overused, throwaway word in our society. Had it always been so disposable? I learned that the word love has existed as long as there has been language. In Hebrew one of the words used for love is "Ahava" which also means "I give." So beautiful and appropriate because to love someone is to give to them the most precious thing you own, yourself. Love is to put another first, to give to them preference to the point of sacrifice. I know Jesus loves me because He said the ultimate "I love you" at the cross. At that time, I wasn't His friend or follower, I wasn't even a person, and yet the Bible says that He was willing to sacrifice Himself to rescue the future me from sin and death. Truly the best love story ever told.

#Jesusmyhero #sacrificiallove #lovedbythekingofkings #iamprecioustogod #actionsandwords #littleseedsofhope

Dear children, let us not love with words or speech but with actions and in truth. 1 John 3:18

Reckless Love by Cory Asbury

DAY 91

Zayden got his report card and Foye called me and gave me a heads up. My son was nervous about mom coming home from work because there are some areas that need significant improvement. Dad already had the heavy discussion, so I got to surprise Zayden and play good cop. I had the privilege of reminding him of who he is: Zayden Belyea, our beloved handsome son, a Young Marine, who is super smart with an amazing memory and who has overcome seemingly insurmountable obstacles at just eleven years old. More importantly, a son of God, rescued from his sins by his big brother Jesus, filled with the Holy Spirit and gifted to do great things for God! Sometimes I feel like Zayden. I've failed in some way and am skulking around, waiting for God to rain down the punishment. I forget that Papa has already seen everything I will ever do and besides that's not how He works. The whole Bible is full of stories where God tells people that He wants to forgive them, all they have to do is take the first step and 'fess up that they've done wrong. Why is that so hard for us, for me to admit to God that I've sinned? God already knows we need grace upon grace. He's omniscient, which means all knowing. I can't hide from Him. Beloved, the only thing Papa God wants to rain upon us is LOVE. Let's have hearts like children, confess our sins, receive forgiveness and dance in the puddles.

#chosenchild #wantedbyGod #perfectlyloved #noskulkingzone
#littleseedsofhope

One thing I ask from the Lord, this only do I seek:
that I may dwell in the house of the Lord all the days of my life to gaze
on the beauty of the Lord and to seek him in his temple. Psalm 27:4

Throne Room by Kim Walker Smith

DAY 92

When I was a new Mom, I joined the missionary committee at church. The very first meeting I went to was held at a nursing home so that a tiny, elderly lady named Ruth could attend. Ruth was a former missionary. She had dedicated her life to God and never married or had children. We went up to her room and found Ruth sitting in bed, hunched and twisted from arthritis, on oxygen, and smiling. Looking around, I noticed a curiously large stack of index cards on the nightstand and nosy me asked what they were for. "Those are prayer requests", she said. "I don't sleep very well because of my arthritis. At night, I go through the cards and pray for people. I can't do much for the Lord because of my body, but I can pray." Beloved, I was immediately convicted. The truth is I had joined the Missionary Committee because it only required my time one day a month. I was looking for the least I could do for God without being inconvenienced. Ruth, on the other hand, was looking for the MOST she could do for God, even in her final days, with her body wracked by illness and infirmity, and she did it with JOY! Jesus, may I serve you and the people you bring into my life as faithfully and joyfully as this tiny powerhouse of a woman.

#neverstoppraying #joyjoyjoyjoy #downinmyheart #littleoldladies
#wisdom #littleseedsofhope

Rejoice always, pray continually, 1 Thessalonians 5:16-17

Make My Life A Prayer To You by Keith Green

DAY 93

I can say in all honesty that God has never let me down. I have had sorrow and pain. I have had happiness and joy. He's walked through it all with me, sometimes pulling me through a dark place kicking and screaming. I could tell you story after story of God's provision in my life, of miracles that I've witnessed, of brokennesses healed. One of my greatest regrets in this life has been the inability to have more children and at 46 years old I've pretty much put that dream to death. I could blame God, but I choose not to because I have seen how my pain has been used to comfort others AND we would probably never have adopted Zayden, who is our son in every way that matters. So my prayer today is that God will grant me a long life, so that I may see more healing, more dark places destroyed, more lives renewed and restored by God's mercy and grace, and that I will be the kind of comfort and friend that Jesus has been for me. Beloved, ask God to open your eyes to where He is moving in YOUR life. Are there areas that you would like Him to transform? Ask Him to help! Good parents are always willing to help their children grow and learn and our Daddy in heaven is no different.

#Amen #46isfabulous #happybirthdaytome #littleseedsofhope

Praise be to the God and Father of our Lord Jesus Christ, the Father of compassion and the God of all comfort, who comforts us in all our troubles, so that we can comfort those in any trouble with the comfort we ourselves receive from God. 2 Corinthians 1:3-4

Just One Touch by Kim Walker-Smith

DAY 94

I love Indian food so I've been asking my coworkers where is the best place to eat in the area. One of the doctors I work with recommended a place to try for lunch but said to be prepared to smell like Indian food for the rest of the day! In other words, everyone would know exactly where I'd been and while some of my coworkers might find the smell appetizing others might be offended. I was at a worship concert where over 26 churches were represented and you could feel the presence of God. I left completely energized. I'm pretty convinced that if you had put me in a dark room I would have glowed. It made me think about Indian food. When we spend time with God, people can tell. There's an aroma of hope and peace about us that smells of the Gospel of Christ. The Bible says that to some the Gospel carries the stench of death and for others it is the sweet fragrance of life (2Cor. 2:16). If the good news is that God loves you like crazy and wants you to become His beloved child smells delicious, then come and feast at Jesus's table! There is no charge, there are no calories, and when you leave, you will be energized and filled with love and hope. Jesus's place is not fancy, you come as you are. No reservations required and shoes are optional.

#bonapetito #lifeordeath #faithhopelove #lovemychurch
#howwouldjesussmell #littleseedsofhope

Better is one day in your courts than a thousand elsewhere;
Psalm 84:10

The Gospel by Ryan Stevenson

DAY 95

It's one of those mornings when my prayer in my journal reads, "Papa, I need help. I need to see You move." The verse below reminds me that if I have nothing but Jesus, He is enough. All of the other things we set our hearts and affections on are secondary blessings. I struggle with this because I want Jesus and.... success, money, a nice house, great cars (you fill in the blanks) etc. etc... While all of these things are GOOD, if I think about it, Jesus is the only lasting thing of value that I really have. I used to manage physician practices. When my staff was having a particularly difficult day, I would remind them that six months from now they're most likely not going to remember this moment and to try to get through it the best they could, actively looking for things to smile about. Today, I am choosing to rest my head on my Papa's chest, worship Him and count both my earthly and heavenly blessings. I am choosing to smile and remember that He is the source of my joy and without Him I would be lost, in every way.

#savedfrommyself #myjoypapa #lookforasmile #worshiphimonly
#littleseedsofhope

And everyone who calls on the name of the Lord will be saved.
Acts 2:21

Blessings by Laura Story

DAY 96

To everyone else, our front porch looks ordinary, however, looks can be deceiving. Every morning Foye sits out there and has coffee with Jesus. If only the neighbors could see Jesus sitting on one of my outdoor chairs, listening as Foye pours out his heart and reads the Bible. It would go viral all over the web. But just because the neighbors can't see Him doesn't make the fact that He is meeting with my husband any less real. I know this because I have watched Foye grow exponentially over the years as a direct result of the time he spends with the Lord each morning. Do you ever think it would be easier to have faith if we could actually see Jesus? I used to think that, but then I remembered all the people that DID see Jesus and not only rejected him but HATED him and sent him to a brutal death on a Roman cross. Why? It's because He didn't fit into their little Jesus box. He did things they didn't think He should do. He loved people they didn't think He should love. He unapologetically challenged their assumptions and their prejudices. Having faith and following Jesus has never ever been easy, even when people could see Him. So why do we do it? I can only share my reasons. Without Jesus I would an anxious, fearful, negative, and compulsive mess. I'd be locked in a room medicating myself with food or worse. If I am kind, or loving or compassionate, it's because of Him. If I have any success in my marriage or with my children, it's because of Him. That's just the short list. If I'm one hundred percent honest, my motivations are selfish. I like the me with Jesus better than the me without. It's as simple as that.

#simplefaith #datewithjesus #coffeetalk #renewyourmind
#littleseedsofhope

Do not conform to the pattern of this world, but be transformed by the renewing of your mind. Then you will be able to test and approve what God's will is—his good, pleasing and perfect will. Romans 12:2

What A Beautiful Name by Hillsong

DAY 97

One night, shortly after Emilie was born, I was startled awake. Have you ever looked through a viewfinder camera? You pull down the lever and the next picture appears. It was as if someone was clicking the lever in front of my eyes over and over again. One second I would see our bedroom and the next, three beings. Two surrounded our bed and one stood in front of Emilie's room across the hall. Menacing evil radiated from the beings in our room. However, in front of Emilie's door was an angelic warrior standing guard. At my scream, Foye also awoke and tried to convince me that I was having a night terror, but the vision would not go away. I started to pray The Lord's Prayer. It was the first thing that came to mind. Within a few seconds everything returned to normal. The next morning I called my pastor completely freaked out! We talked about how there is a spiritual battle taking place. All around, unseen forces are fighting for AND against us, but we are not powerless. Jesus has sent the Holy Spirit who helps us pray, encourages us and even intercedes on our behalf. When I am in a situation that can be potentially dangerous, like crossing a busy street, I pull Zayden close to my side so that I can protect him from harm. Beloved, ALL OF LIFE is full of danger. On that day, Papa was reminding me that Satan wants to destroy marriages and we needed to stick so close to the Holy Spirit's side it looks like we are in a three legged race. Beloved, have you prepared for the battle today?

#spiritualwarfare #faithnotfear #prayerkaratechop #takethatsatan
#littleseedsofhope

So I say, walk by the Spirit,
and you will not gratify the desires of the flesh. Galatians 5:16

Walk By Faith by Jeremy Camp

DAY 98

My first college semester I was on academic probation for poor grades. I managed to get through two more years and then I quit to get married. It wasn't until several years later that I decided to try again. I had no confidence in myself so I did something a little crazy, I enrolled in a CALCULUS class at our local college! I struggled in math, so I thought that if I could conquer calculus, then I could do ANYTHING. My old ways of dodging homework and cramming for the test weren't going to fly. I even signed up for tutoring. In the end I got a B! I know, it's a miracle! Sometimes, we live the Christian life like we're cramming for a course. We don't spend time reading the Bible, listening to worship music or praying until we are in a jam and then we wonder why our faith and our relationship with Papa is...meh. It doesn't have to be that way. Start small. Remember how three minutes a day changed ME. You could read the gospel of John or pick a Bible verse and challenge yourself to memorize it. You could listen to worship music on your way to work. In my life those small steps have made a HUGE difference and turned my "meh" faith into a vibrant relationship with God. Beloved, baby steps are precious to parents. We hold our breath for them. We want to capture them on our phones and share them with all of our friends. Do you think Papa God is any different?

#ineedatshirt #isurvivedcalculus #babysteps #wecandoit #littleseedsofhope

All Scripture is God-breathed and is useful for teaching, rebuking, correcting and training in righteousness, so that the servant of God may be thoroughly equipped for every good work.
2 Timothy 3:16-17

All I Ever Wanted by Margaret Becker

DAY 99

We were at my friend Heather's house for a dinner party and Emilie noticed a picture on a shelf. It was the day that Heather and I graduated from nursing school. We are both wearing white nursey outfits and smiling. Emilie said, "Mom, I wasn't sure you would like the picture because it was before you lost weight, but I think you looked beautiful." Beloved, did you ever have a pair of tinted sunglasses that makes the world look pink or blue? When I first looked at that graduation picture, I had the old Maria's tinted grey, judgy, self-demeaning glasses. Through them I saw a woman full of guilt and shame, a woman who despised herself for turning to food instead of God when she was anxious or worried. I saw a woman who HATED the fact that her dress was white and would make her look even fatter. I confess, it took me a minute to even realize I had those nasty glasses on. Once I did, I whipped them OFF and SMUSHED them under my foot! In their place I put on my Jesus Loves ME, rosy tinted, sparkly Princess shades. I took a look at that same picture and saw as woman who had accomplished an incredibly hard goal. Yes! I saw a compassionate woman with a heart to serve people who was sharing a wonderful milestone with a beloved friend. I saw a BEAUTIFUL WOMAN upon whom Jesus wanted to shower His love and forgiveness, mercy and grace! I LOVE THAT PICTURE!!! I am going to ask her for a copy.

#freedom #nocondemnationinChrist #breakeverychain #thankyouJesus
#littleseedsofhope

Here is a trustworthy saying that deserves full acceptance: Christ Jesus came into the world to save sinners—of whom I am the worst.
1 Timothy 1:15

You Say by Lauren Daigle

DAY 100

When I was a little girl my cousins and I would put on shows for our parents in the living room. We'd huddle in the basement all day and declare it a no grown-ups zone while we practiced our routines. Finally, it was showtime! Without any fear of rejection we would sing and dance our hearts out. Our parents would ooh and ahhh, clap loudly and tell us how wonderful we were. I really miss those days. As an adult I have a lot of insecurities. I'm a messy-vert. That's a word I made up because sometimes I'm an extrovert, and sometimes I'm an introvert. My life is messy and does not fit into neat and tidy little boxes. You probably don't know this, but I can get really nervous before I lead worship on a Sunday. I am my own worst critic and often the voices in my head say things like, "You're too old to do this. You're not spiritual enough. You're not talented enough. You don't deserve to be up there." Then the music starts, and the joy of the Lord fills my heart and drowns out the lies of the Enemy. Everyone watching sees a forty-something year old woman. They don't realize that in that moment, I am eight years old again. I've been transported to Papa God's living room and He is watching me sing just for Him. I have no fear because I am perfectly loved, perfectly accepted and He is laughing, eyes dancing, full of JOY because of ME! Friend, you don't have to be the worship leader to dance and sing for Papa God. My sweet Foye inspires me. Even though he can't carry a tune in a paper bag, he is not shy about belting out a praise song. He sings his heart out because he knows who his audience is and Daddy doesn't care about perfect pitch. Papa God is listening for the sound of a heart in tune with His. That's the sweetest music there is. So Beloved, turn on that praise music, drown out the lies and with abandon, with joy, and with hope, lift your voice and SING because it's showtime!

#myhappyplace #danceforjesus #ohhowhelovesus #littleseedsofhope

How great you are, Sovereign Lord! There is no one like you, and there is no God but you, as we have heard with our own ears. 2 Samuel 7:22

Great Are You Lord by All Sons and Daughters

SCRIPTURE REFERENCES

Deuteronomy 7:9 .... Day 54

Joshua 1:8 .... Day 18

I Samuel 2:2 .... Day 36

2 Samuel 7:22 .... Day 100

Psalm 1: 1-2 .... Day 17

Psalm 27:4 .... Day 91

Psalm 32:8 .... Day 43

Psalm 33:18 .... Day 6

Psalm 34:18 .... Day 64

Psalm 51: 1-2 .... Day 62

Psalm 51:10 .... Day 48

Psalm 55:22 .... Day 4

Psalm 56: 3 .... Day 85

Psalm 60:12 .... Day 23

Psalm 68:5 .... Day 29

Psalm 68:19 .... Day 39

Psalm 84:10 .... Day 94

Psalm 94:19 .... Day 76

Psalm 115:14 .... Day 52

Psalm 119:105 .... Day 71

Psalm 119:114 .... Day 2

Psalm 121:2 .... Day 58

Proverbs 1:7 .... Day 45

Proverbs 3:5 .... Day 79

Proverbs 15:1 .... Day 72

Proverbs 16:9 .... Day 69

Proverbs 17:28 .... Day 81

Proverbs 21:7 .... Day 14

Proverbs 21:21 .... Day 49

Proverbs 31:30 .... Day 10

Ecclesiastes 7:9 .... Day 15

Isaiah 26:3 .... Day 59

Isaiah 40:28 .... Day 87

Isaiah 40:31 .... Day 60

Isaiah 41:13 .... Day 7

Isaiah 42:18 .... Day 73

Isaiah 43: 2 .... Day 5

Isaiah 48: 17 .... Day 63

Isaiah 49:6 .... Day 8

Jeremiah 32:17 .... Day 33

Ezekiel 36:26 .... Day 42

Matthew 6:25 .... Day 44

Matthew 11:28 .... Day 67

Matthew 28:6 .... Day 83

Luke 1:37 .... Day 32

Luke 24:51 .... Day 51

John 1:9 .... Day 56

John 3:16 .... Day 70

John 3:30 .... Day 25

John 5:24 .... Day 65

John 6:35 .... Day 13

John 11:25 .... Day 78

John 14:21 .... Day 86

John 14:27 .... Day 24

John 15:5 .... Day 20

John 16:33 .... Day 53

Acts 1:8.................................Day 41

Acts 2:21..............................Day 95

Romans 8:1-2........................Day 88

Romans 8:11.........................Day 84

Romans 10:9.........................Day 82

Romans 12:2.........................Day 96

Romans 15:4.........................Day 57

2 Corinthians 1:3-4.......Day 93

2 Corinthians 4:16.........Day 61

2 Corinthians 5:21.........Day 16

Galatians 5:16.....................Day 97

Galatians 6:7........................Day 9

Galatians 2:20.....................Day 50

Ephesians 3:20....................Day 68

Ephesians 4:32....................Day 1

Ephesians 4:29....................Day 35

Ephesians 5:2.......................Day 21

Ephesians 5:26....................Day 3

Philippians 2:13.................Day 66

Philippians 4:6....................Day 37

Colossians 3:17...................Day 74

Colossians 3:13...................Day 30

Colossians 4:6.....................Day 37

1 Thessalonians 5:16-17
....Day 92

1 Timothy 1:15....................Day 99

1 Timothy 4:12....................Day 12

2 Timothy 1:7.......................Day 22

2 Timothy 3:16-17............Day 98

Titus 2:11-12........................Day 40

Hebrews 4:16.......................Day 28

Hebrews 11:6.......................Day 11

Hebrews 13:16....................Day 80

James 1:12.............................Day 55

James 1:19.............................Day 75

James 4:7................................Day 38

James 5:16.............................Day 89

1 Peter 2:9.............................Day 19

1 Peter 3:12..........................Day 31

1 Peter 5:6.............................Day 46

1 Peter 5:8.............................Day 26

1 John 1:9..............................Day 34

1 John 2:2..............................Day 27

1 John 3:18............................Day 90

Revelation 1:8.....................Day 77

TOPICAL & SONG INDEX

Abandoned	Day 2	*You Are Not Alone* by Kari Jobe
	Day 85	*Do It Again* by Elevation Worship
Abiding	Day 20	*He's Always Been Faithful* by Sara Groves
Anger	Day 15	*Mended* by Matthew West
Anxiety	Day 47	*Cast My Cares* by Finding Favor
	Day 67	*Carry Me* by Josh Wilson
Attitudes	Day 74	*Joy* by For King and Country
Blessings	Day 95	*Blessings* by Laura Story
Burdened	Day 65	*Just Come In* by Margaret Becker
Caring	Day 80	*You Are For Me* by Kari Jobe
Cleansing	Day 61	*White As Snow* by John Foreman
Conviction	Day 71	*God with Us* by Jesus Culture
Devotion	Day 18	*Lord I Need You* by Matt Maher
Direction	Day 63	*Cry Out To Jesus* by Third Day
Discouragement	Day 64	*There is Power* by Lincoln Brewster
Failure	Day 6	*Break Every Chain* by Jesus Culture
	Day 28	*Broken Things* by Matthew West
Faith	Day 11	*Jesus I Believe* by Big Daddy Weave
	Day 31	*Give Me Faith* by Elevation Worship
	Day 33	*Even If* by Mercy Me
	Day 39	*Let Faith Arise* by Bridge City
	Day 46	*Good Good Father* by Chris Tomlin
	Day 78	*Mention Of Your Name* by Bethel Music
	Day 96	*What A Beautiful Name* by Hillsong
	Day 97	*Walk By Faith* by Jeremy Camp
	Day 98	*All I Ever Wanted* by Margaret Becker
Family	Day 19	*Who You Say I Am* by Hillsong

Forgiveness	Day 29	*Mighty To Save* by Laura Story
	Day 30	*Forgiven* by Crowder
	Day 34	*Jesus Friend Of Sinners* by Casting Crowns
	Day 48	*Freedom Hymn* by Austin French
	Day 62	*O Come to the Altar* by Elevation Worship
	Day 75	*New Wine* by Hillsong
	Day 91	*Throne Room* by Kim Walker Smith
Friendship	Day 1	*Simple Gospel* by United Pursuit
	Day 52	*Love Has a Name* by Jesus Culture
Fruitfulness	Day 17	*My Simple Prayer* by Maria Belyea
Gospel	Day 94	*Gospel* by Ryan Stevenson
Grace	Day 88	*Who You Say I AM* by Hillsong
Health	Day 14	*The More I Seek You* by Kari Jobe
Helper	Day 57	*Overcomer* by Mandissa
	Day 58	*Short To The North* by Robin Mark
	Day 59	*I Need Thee Every Hour* by Jars of Clay
	Day 68	*Holy Spirit* by Francesca Batistelli
Holy Spirit	Day 40	*Spirit Of The Living God* by Vertical Worship
Humility	Day 37	*Give Me Your Eyes* by Brandon Heath
	Day 83	*Chain Breaker* by Zach Williams
Insight	Day 73	*Amazing Grace My Chains Are Gone* by Chris Tomlin
Kindness	Day 9	*King Of My Heart* by Bethel Music
	Day 10	*By Our Love* by Christy Nockles
	Day 35	*If We Are The Body* by Casting Crowns
Light	Day 56	My Lighthouse by Rend Collective
Likeness	Day 84	To Live Is Christ by Sidewalk Prophets

Living Word   Day 3   *In Christ Alone* by Passion
Love   Day 7   How He Loves by David Crowder Band

                  Day 90   *Reckless Love* by Cory Asbury
Mission   Day 21   I Will Follow by Chris Tomlin
Motivation   Day 23   *Run* by Paul Coleman
Peace   Day 24   *Tremble* by Mosaic

                  Day 44   *Prince of Peace* by Hillsong United
Perseverance   Day 5   *Champion* by Brian and Katie Torwalt

                  Day 55   *Courageous* by Casting Crowns

                  Day 57   *Overcomer* by Mandisa

                  Day 72   *Mountain* by Brian and Katie Torwalt
Praise   Day 100   *Great Are You Lord* by
                             All Sons and Daughters
Prayer   Day 82   *Give Me Jesus* by Jeremy Camp

                  Day 89   *Prince of Peace* by Hillsong United

                  Day 92   *Make My Life A Prayer To You* by
                             Kieth Green
Regret   Day 66   *Come As You Are* by Crowder
Relationship   Day 54   *Beautiful Jesus* by Jonathan and
                             Melissa Helser
Remember   Day 60   *Fierce* by Jesus Culture
Renewal   Day 42   *Set A Fire* by United Pursuit

                  Day 49   *I Am* by Crowder
Rest   Day 87   *It Is Well* by Bethel Music
Righteousness   Day 16   *Garment of Praise* by Robin Mark
Sacrifice   Day 27   Above All by Michael W. Smith
Satisfied   Day 13   *King of My Heart* by Bethel Music

                  Day 36   *Build My Life* by Housefires
Scars   Day 8   *Less Like Scars* by Sara Groves
Sharing   Day 76   *Leave Your Sins At The Door* by
                             Maria Belyea

Sin	Day 25	*Born Again* by Austin French
	Day 45	*You Alone Can Rescue* by Matt Redman
Stubbornness	Day 43	*Jesus Take The Wheel* by Carrie Underwood
Strength	Day 22	*Fierce* by Jesus Culture
Temptation	Day 4	*Lose My Soul* by Toby Mac
	Day 38	*Broken Vessels/Amazing Grace* by Hillsong
Testimony	Day 12	*My Story* by Big Daddy Weave
	Day 32	*God Of All My Days* Casting Crowns
	Day 41	*Testify* by Need to Breathe
	Day 51	*This Is Home* by Switchfoot
Transformation	Day 93	*Just One Touch* by Kim Walker-Smith
	Day 26	*Run Devil Run* by Crowder
	Day 99	*You Say* by Lauren Daigle
Treasures	Day 77	*Diamonds* by Hawk Nelson
Trust	Day 50	*Trust In You* by Lauren Daigle
	Day 69	*Oceans* by Hillsong United
	Day 70	*How Can It Be* by Lauren Daigle
	Day 79	*Fearless* by Jasmine Murray
Uncertainty	Day 86	*Need You Now* by Plumb
Usefulness	Day 81	*Dry Bones* by Lauren Daigle
Worry	Day 53	*White Flag* by Passion feat. Chris Tomlin